Praise for *The Joys*

Insight and Wisdom from the Jewish Tradition

"A must-read for anyone who loves a child and wants to be the best parent they can be. *The Joys & Oys of Parenting* helps us fulfill the most important role of our lives—raise good people who can thrive someday without us. For a better world, I hope every parent has a copy on their nightstand."

—**Michele Borba, EdD,** educational psychologist and author of
UnSelfie: Why Empathetic Kids Succeed in Our All-About-Me World

"Parenting is one of the most challenging but gratifying roles in one's life. *The Joys & Oys of Parenting* will serve as a wonderful resource for parents, grandparents, and other caregivers. It highlights realistic and practical strategies for nurturing such important qualities in children as kindness, empathy, generosity, motivation, responsibility, gratitude, and resilience— qualities that are essential for well-being throughout our lives. While the book is rooted in Judaic traditions, the wisdom it imparts is applicable for parents regardless of their faith or beliefs."

—**Robert Brooks, PhD,** Harvard Medical School, co-author of
*Raising Resilient Children: Fostering Strength, Hope, and
Optimism in Your Child* and *Raising a Self-Disciplined Child: Help
Your Child Become More Responsible, Confident, and Resilient*

"Parenting is indeed a 'sacred mission' and this book reminds us that the sacred wisdom of Judaism can help us make sense of everything from sibling rivalries, to bedtime stories, to finding rest. Parents of all faiths will be amazed by the practicality of Jewish tradition just as they will be drawn into the freshness of the ancient calls to wholeness, to peace, to goodness, and to love. I'm not Jewish by birth, but that didn't stop me from learning and growing in the reading."

—**Timothy Shriver, PhD,** *Chair, Special Olympics; cofounder of CASEL (Collaborative for Academic, Social, and Emotional Learning)*

"The Joys & Oys of Parenting is accessible and informed by both child development and Jewish perspectives. At any stage of parenting, parents will appreciate both the kernels of wisdom and the reassurance that they are not in it alone."

—**Stephanie Fink,** Union for Reform Judaism, Associate Director of Engaging Families with Young Children

"This is a refreshing, modern look at raising Jewish children, with common sense approaches based in tradition. The practical tips offered to everyday parenting challenges are insightful, creative, and totally doable! Who knew tackling everything from laundry woes to teaching gratitude to a toddler could be covered in one book? With real-life, modern approaches to using Jewish values and stories to raise amazing Jewish adults, *The Joys & Oys of Parenting* is a gift to any parent—newbie or veteran."

—**Amy Bergman,** Director of Jewish Family Life, Friedman Commission for Jewish Education; Engagement Officer, PJ Library

"A positive and inspiring book, *The Joys & Oys of Parenting* presents realistic examples of the challenges all parents face, and provides reliable guidance from wise and loving experts on ways to work through them. When you buy a gift for a new baby, add a copy of this book for its parents!"

—**Cheryl R. Finkel,** leadership consultant and former head of the Epstein School, Atlanta

The Joys & Oys of Parenting

Dear Scout,

We know it's your plan to give your parents + grandma lots of joy. But you know how these adults can be. So we suggest you leave this book around where they can see it, so they give you less oy, + you can give them more joy!

With much love,

Ellen + Maurice

The Joys & Oys of Parenting

Insight and Wisdom from the Jewish Tradition

by Maurice J. Elias, PhD; Marilyn E. Gootman, EdD;
and Heather L. Schwartz, MA

Foreword by Rabbi Kerry Olitzky

BEHRMAN HOUSE
www.behrmanhouse.com

Design: Annemarie Redmond
Cover design: Terry Taylor
Project editors: Tzivia MacLeod, Dena Neusner
Cover art direction: Ann D. Koffsky

Published by Behrman House, Inc.
Springfield, New Jersey 07081
www.behrmanhouse.com

ISBN 978-0-87441-942-9

The publisher gratefully acknowledges the following sources:
Cover images from Shutterstock.com: HorenkO (textures), wongwean (figures at top), advent (man), poosan (woman)

Excerpt(s) from THE GREAT PARTNERSHIP: SCIENCE, RELIGION, AND THE SEARCH FOR MEANING by Rabbi Jonathan Sacks, copyright © 2011 by Jonathan Sacks. Used by permission of Schocken Books, an imprint of the Knopf Doubleday Publishing Group, a division of Penguin Random House LLC. All rights reserved.

Excerpt from "How to Spoil the Pleasure of Learning," by Tessa Livingstone, *The Guardian*, April 22, 2008, courtesy of Guardian News & Media Ltd.

Five humor tips that spell "LAUGH" used with permission of Dr. Ed Dunkelblau, director of the Institute for Emotionally Intelligent Learning.

Library of Congress Cataloging-in-Publication Data
Names: Elias, Maurice J., author. | Gootman, Marilyn E., 1944– author. |
    Schwartz, Heather L., author.
Title: The joys & oys of parenting : insight and wisdom from the Jewish
    tradition / by Maurice J. Elias, PhD, Marilyn E. Gootman, EdD, and Heather
    L. Schwartz, MA ; foreword by Rabbi Kerry Olitzky.
Description: Springfield, NJ : Behrman House, 2016. | Includes
    bibliographical references.
Identifiers: LCCN 2016020319 | ISBN 9780874419429 (pbk.)
Subjects: LCSH: Child rearing. | Child rearing—Religious aspects—Judaism. |
    Parenting—Religious aspects—Judaism. | Parent and child (Jewish law) |
    Children—Conduct of life.
Classification: LCC HQ769.3 .E55 2016 | DDC 649/.1—dc23 LC record available at
https://lccn.loc.gov/2016020319

Printed in the United States of America

Visit www.behrmanhouse.com/joys-of-parenting for more resources.

Dedication

For Rabbi Yakov Hilsenrath, z"l, who first introduced me
to Jewish parenting education classes ("PEP") in the 1980s and whose
wisdom has found its way into many pages of this book; and for my
grandsons, Harry Elijah Stopek and Isaac Ferris Stopek, who provide
me with endless joy, love, new learning, and foobadoos.

—MJE

For my grandmother, Anna Kachelnick Pransky,
who sparked within me a lifelong love of Judaism and all that it has to
offer. For my precious children and grandchildren, who are a continuous
source of joy. And for my husband, Elliot, the best partner I could imagine
for navigating the challenges and wonders of parenting.

—MG

For my mother, whose beauty has left the earth but whose
essence and fortitude live on in me; every good thing I am as a mother is
rooted in her love and values. For my father, whose resilience, strength,
and loyalty have made our lives infinitely fuller and more meaningful.
And for my four boys, who make it all worth it.

—HS

Table of Contents

Foreword

Judaism has something to say about everything—and not just in the synagogue or on holidays. Perhaps that is one of the reasons why some scholars, like the twentieth-century thinker Rabbi Mordecai Kaplan, called Judaism a civilization rather than simply a religion. He felt that the word "religion" was too narrow and limiting. Judaism encompassed much more, including language, literature, land, food…and wisdom. Kaplan also referred to Judaism as peoplehood, noting that over the course of their long history the Jewish people accumulated folk wisdom as they wandered the world, encountering the values of many host countries and cultures.

It comes as no surprise, therefore, that Judaism has something to say about parenting too, offering wisdom that extends beyond the Jewish people into the global marketplace of ideas. Some wisdom is hard to access. And some books are hard to access as well. But Jewish parenting wisdom should be available to all those who seek it. *The Joys & Oys of Parenting* captures this Jewish world wisdom and makes it accessible to everyone, regardless of religious background or family structure.

While those who have an extensive Jewish background will find much meaning in this book and have a rich experience in reading it because of their background, the wisdom in these pages doesn't depend on Jewish literacy as an entry point. The doors to Jewish thought are open to all who want to enter: parents from all sectors of the Jewish community, adoptive parents, stepparents, grandparents, non-Jewish parents in interfaith marriages, Jewish parents whose religious upbringing is limited, single parents who are looking for additional guidance, and even grandparents from other religious backgrounds whose adult children are raising Jewish children. For all those who want to know what Judaism has to say about parenting, whether or not they have a personal stake in it, there is much wisdom in these pages, as well.

Those of us who are parents know that it is sometimes difficult to see or remember the joys of parenting in the midst of its difficulties. One thing that I like to remind myself as a parent—something that I learned from the passage of the ancient Israelites through the desert—is that the joy is in the journey. And parenthood certainly *is* a journey, with all of its up and downs. It is this insight that carried me through my own parenting journey and continues to do so now that I am a grandparent. And the authors of this book make sure that the joy, and Judaism's lasting values, are not lost on the trip going forth—even through the desert.

Jewish thinkers have devoted much of their wisdom to parenting because Judaism takes everyday parenting tasks—even those that are routine and exhausting—and raises them to the level of the sacred. Parenting itself is not just given over to those who have children. Parenting is a privilege, an honor, a goal to be reached. Parenting is part of the covenantal relationship that is established at birth with those who have given the child life or agreed to raise the child as their own. We willingly enter this covenant and are bound by it. The same is true for adoptive parents and stepparents—and parents whose children came to them through the miracles of science—which is why Judaism considers those who raise children more important than those who gave birth to them. The ancient Jewish philosopher Philo of Alexandria went so far as to say, "What God is to the world, parents are to their children." Regardless of one's theology or the place of God in one's life, the sentiment is clear: as far as Judaism is concerned, there is no greater honor or responsibility than being a parent to children.

Parenting wisdom doesn't exist in a vacuum. It doesn't emerge from a group of people sitting in an academic setting, posing questions and answers and thinking about what it is to be a parent. Instead, Jewish parenting wisdom emerges from what Rabbi Irwin Kula likes to call "the sacred messiness of life." This was as true for the ancient Rabbis as it is for us today. The wisdom in this book comes from Jewish tradition, the training and education of the authors, and the authors' own personal experiences as parents, with all of the joys and the messiness.

One of the chief lessons of Jewish parenting wisdom is the importance of shaping Jewish identity for your children by creating Jewish memories—and you, the reader, are the primary source for such memories. Sometimes we are lucky and good things just happen. Those unplanned happenings become positive memories that are etched into the psyche of our children. But we don't want to bank the future on such happenstance. More often, we are wise to plan activities with wisdom and insight, guided by our values, and it is these activities that become the memories that our children bring into adulthood. It is these memories that help to form and shape their evolving Jewish identity—religious or secular—in whatever form it takes. As our children grow, they may someday apply what they have learned to their own children—thus contributing to the reservoir of Jewish parenting wisdom. Their children may do the same for those who come after. And we are all enriched as a result.

Rabbi Kerry M. Olitzky
Executive Director, Big Tent Judaism

Introduction

L et's look back to a time when we were still just thinking about having children. Many of us wondered what
kind of parents we would be and how our children
would behave as we were raising them. We had preconceived
ideas—maybe even hopes—about how our kids would look, how
politely they would act, and, of course, how loving and affection-
ate they would be with us and with each other. Our hopes fueled
by popular culture and perhaps upbeat glimpses of our friends'
kids, many of us felt confident about the constant joys that parenting would bring.

Then we actually became parents. Our preconceptions and
hopes were quickly tempered by the day-to-day reality of parenting. It's certainly full of love and joy, but also full of confusion,
exhaustion, and exasperation. Oy! Parenting, we quickly learned,
might be the most difficult thing we would ever do.

It's in those tough moments that we need the most hope—
the hope that as parents, we won't just survive but will do

our jobs well, raising children who not only will make good lives for themselves but will also leave the world a better place. Imagine the hope and joy of that, of growing our children into amazing adults.

But that joy in parenting—those precious moments of what many Jews refer to as *nachas,* or parental pride—doesn't have to wait for later in life when our kids are grown. There are joys and proud "parent moments" that we can hold on to and cherish right now. Along with all the worry, pressure, and challenges that come with parenting, we can delight in our kids as they fill our hearts like nothing else. But we can't lose sight of the greater goal: guiding our children into becoming competent and productive adults. That won't just happen because we love them; we need to dig in and do the messy, not-so-fun stuff, working at it until we—and our kids—get it right.

So we need guidance. Where can we find it? For Jewish parents or for parents looking for Jewish insight and inspiration, our faith's thousands of years' worth of wisdom offers beliefs and values that have proved successful, generation after generation. Judaism offers us clear guidance and specific principles for raising children into successful, productive, confident, secure, and charitable adults—adults who do more than just survive but also manage to thrive in this world.

Beginning with the concept of *shalom bayit* (a peaceful home) as a foundation, our family lives can be defined and distinguished by peace, respect, and loving-kindness (*chesed*). We can use Jewish teachings in our daily lives as guidance for raising our children. And infusing our homes with these values will increase the likelihood that our children will adopt and apply them in their own lives as they navigate the complex world in which we live.

We, Maurice, Marilyn, and Heather, were inspired to write this book by our own experiences in the trenches of parenting. Jewish wisdom and perspective have helped each of us to navigate family life and have empowered us in the face of daily challenges. Two of us, Maurice and Marilyn, have grown children, and now grandchildren, and have spent much of our careers working with children, parents, families, and schools. Heather is still in the hands-on stage, raising four children and working with students both in primary school and at the university level. We are all directly involved in education, using our degrees and expertise to work with children and young adults at every developmental stage—from young ones all the way through the college years.

While we come from varying backgrounds of Jewish experience and Jewish education, we share the common commitment to passing on treasured elements of our heritage. We've seen how tradition has added meaning and joy to the lives of our own families, and those of countless others around us, both religious and nonreligious.

We realize that practicing intentional parenting, making conscious, deliberate, and value-based parenting choices, from a Jewish perspective (or any other perspective) can be challenging. But we believe the rewards are worth the investment: raising children who leave a meaningful mark on this world and inspire others to do the same. We're excited to pass on the wonder and beauty of our Jewish tradition to you and your families. Along with the "oy," we want to be sure you don't miss out on the joy.

This book explores cherished concepts in Jewish parenting, demonstrating how relevant they still are in today's overscheduled, technologically advanced world. These basic elements, like security, peacefulness, resilience, kindness, thankfulness, responsibility, and motivation, can be strengthened with time-honored Jewish beliefs and traditions.

The Fundamental Questions Parents Ask

Being a parent involves asking fundamental questions about how to raise a child into a confident, successful adult—questions like:

- How can I create a peaceful home?

- How can I help my child feel more secure?

- How can I empower my child to face life's challenges?

- How can I teach my child responsibility?

- How can I motivate my child to succeed?

- How can I guide my child to be kind?

- How can I inspire my child to be appreciative?

Each chapter of this book is dedicated to answering one of these questions, offering specific guidance that can be applied in any home, while drawing on the rich and enduring principles of Judaism.

- Chapter one looks at creating a peaceful home environment, building stronger bonds between family members by strengthening the skills of listening and interacting with each other, and dealing with sibling rivalry.

- Chapter two explores providing our children with stability and security through ordinary activities like creating schedules, eating together as a family, and celebrating family traditions and our heritage.

- Chapter three looks at building resilience in a complicated world and teaches specific attitudes and behaviors that help our children "bounce back" and thrive, even under adversity.

- Chapter four digs into taking responsibility, presenting our kids with skills and behaviors that will benefit them throughout life, in relationships, and in school, work, and other areas.

- Chapter five examines how to encourage our children to be self-motivated, giving them the confidence they need to realize and actualize their full potential.

- Chapter six provides tips for developing values and participating in activities that will help our children see the world beyond themselves and foster a spirit of kindness.

- Chapter seven focuses on cultivating in our children gratitude and thankfulness, making them a constant part of life and family interaction so they will grow as part of our children's lasting character.

Each chapter lays out practical ideas and ways to apply them that will help children grow into caring, generous, moral, and secure adults, adults who have a strong sense of identity and self-confidence and who are committed to making the world a better place.

Parenting is a sacred mission, full of joys and *oys*, moments in which we wonder if we've taken a wrong turn. But it's ultimately a calling that provides deep fulfillment and satisfaction.

Of course, parenting—even intentional Jewish parenting— doesn't come down to a series of calculated strategies. Ultimately, the flavor and substance of life created in your home is what will connect and bond your family. This book will help you to create everyday household routines inspired by Jewish principles, allow- ing you to tap into enduring, proven ways of creating a home—for your children and for yourself—that nurtures and fulfills your entire family. It's a journey of love, community, tradition, and principles. Let's take it together.

Chapter 1

The Peaceful Home

"A house is built with wisdom, and it is established with understanding.
With knowledge, the rooms are filled with all riches, precious and pleasant."

—*Proverbs 24:3–4*

"Step with care and great tact
and remember that Life's a Great Balancing Act."

—*Dr. Seuss,* Oh, the Places You'll Go!

■ ■ ■

The household is in an uproar. Everyone is upset at everyone else.
There is yelling, no one is listening...and the doorbell rings. It's a
neighbor. Suddenly, everyone calms down; they're not only polite
to the neighbor but also to one another. When the neighbor leaves,
lo and behold, life goes back to something more like "normal," and
the argument is left behind.

■ ■ ■

We call this the "Neighbor Test." It shows that we all value having a peaceful home, but it's easy to lose sight of that ideal. Yet the presence of a neighbor somehow engages our better temperaments and behavior. But we don't have to wait for the lucky arrival of neighbors to create more peace in our homes.

When you think back to images of parenting you had before you became a parent, what comes to mind? Did you imagine little girls sitting around in adorable dresses playing with sweet dolls? Little boys, sweetly hugging your neck and calmly sitting in your lap? The image of a snotty-nosed, screaming toddler lying on the floor of the grocery store refusing to move or of a teenager coming home and locking himself in his room without even a "hello" wasn't exactly what any of us had in mind.

Dreaming of loving and peaceful parenting moments helped us anticipate the joy of having children. But as parents, we now understand that it's up to us to *create* an environment that fosters all the love and peace and joy we'd imagined. An environment that is calm enough, well paced enough, and flexible enough that we have the time, and the intellectual and emotional capacity, to experience those joys. So we look for advice from blogs, books, or anywhere else that might guide us toward more peaceful and loving environments that will help make life more enjoyable and less stressful. But is this even possible? Can a home be calm and stress-free with kids running around creating chaos by just being kids?

A central concept in building an intentional Jewish home is shalom bayit, which literally means "peace of the house." Peace, at home? Who wouldn't want that? Our home should be a safe haven, a place where we feel grounded in respect, comfort, rest, and joy. But that doesn't just happen; to create and sustain a peaceful home requires security, consistency, and harmony.

What does this look like in reality? Is it soft lights, glowing candles, and calm meditation? Is it behavioral—no conflict and all "Kumbaya"? Is it always quiet because the kids are super obedient? Even if we could possibly achieve that, is it really what we want? Most importantly, is it what we want for our kids as they grow up?

Peaceful homes come in many shapes, sizes, and activity and noise levels. What they all share is that sense of shalom bayit, a sense of respect, care, and compassion. Relationships are the key. When there is peace in our relationships at home, we are united, connected, and bonded together as one unit.

While there is nothing uniquely Jewish about wanting a peaceful home, Judaism has a wealth of principles and practices that help us develop relationships to effectively pursue that goal.

Stephen R. Covey writes in *The 7 Habits of Highly Effective People*, "When it comes to developing character strength, inner security and unique personal and interpersonal talents and skills in a child, no institution can or ever will compare with, or effectively substitute for, the home's potential for positive influence."

Our kids learn more from watching us than we realize (or maybe even want to admit), which is underscored by parenting catchphrases like "values are caught, not taught." We know that babies and toddlers initially learn almost everything by copying the actions and behaviors of the people around them. But even older kids take cues from us when it comes to social interaction and relationships. We are their single biggest influence, right through adolescence and beyond.

In the classic children's story *Caps for Sale: A Tale of a Peddler, Some Monkeys and Their Monkey Business*, by Esphyr Slobodkina, a peddler goes from village to village selling caps, wearing his entire inventory piled high on his head. One day, with the caps still on his head, the peddler sits down under a tree to take a nap. When he wakes up, he realizes that monkeys in the tree have taken all but one of his caps, and he's angry about it. So he shakes his finger at the monkeys, but the monkeys only mimic him by shaking their fingers back. He then stamps his feet demanding the caps, but the monkeys only stamp their feet back at him. The peddler finally throws his own cap down to the ground, and what do you know, the monkeys throw their caps down as well. The peddler then retrieves all the caps and goes merrily on his way.

How does this play out in your home with your little "monkeys"? Which of your behaviors are they mimicking?

The first step in creating peace in our homes is to remember that we are always being observed, that our own behaviors are sinking into our children's minds and values. We parents create the atmosphere and sensitivity at home that play a big part in creating a climate of peace or of conflict.

In this chapter we will dive into the fundamental topic of creating a peaceful home through communication with our children and with each other. We'll explore how Jewish teachings help us build an environment that lets us pause and breathe in those moments of pure joy that come with family.

In this chapter, we will explore four everyday principles you can use to bring your family closer together and create bonds to last a lifetime. All are rooted in Jewish teachings.

- Listen skillfully and carefully

- Communicate respectfully

- Express anger constructively

- Minimize sibling rivalry

These four principles will benefit our children today, smooth out our daily routines, and help produce effective, competent people capable of shining light wherever they go in the world.

Listen skillfully and carefully

There's a great *Calvin and Hobbes* cartoon by Bill Watterson that shows Calvin, a boy of around six, standing outside the house and yelling to his mother, "Momm! Hey, Mom!" His mother yells back, "Calvin, stop yelling across the house! If you want to talk to me, walk over to the living room, where I am!" Calvin walks into the house—across the nice, clean carpet—and tells his mom, "I stepped in dog doo. Where's the hose?"

It sure can be a mess sometimes when we don't listen! Good listening is the first step toward effective communication, problem solving, and good relationships—and thus toward a peaceful home. Listening involves receiving information, understanding what is being said, remembering, and responding.

We all want to feel heard. When people listen to us, we feel like what we have to say is important and of value. When they don't, we feel misunderstood and frustrated. Author and teacher Dr. Rachel Naomi Remen has written that "the most important thing we ever give each other is our attention....The most basic and powerful way to connect to another person is to listen. Just listen."

The great first-century rabbi Hillel shaped many Jewish laws and customs. Why were Hillel's teachings so influential? Because he was known for always listening to both sides of an argument before making a decision. A classic story in the spirit of Hillel tells of a rabbi who was sorting out a dispute between two congregants. The first one told his story, and the rabbi said, "That makes a lot of sense." The second one told his story, and the rabbi paused for a moment and said, "That makes a lot of sense." A third person, brought in as an impartial witness, could not keep silent. "Rabbi, you said they both made sense. How can that be?" Without any hesitation, the rabbi replied, "That makes a lot of sense!" He had listened and heard and understood where each was coming from. When this rabbi finally arrived at a decision, no one doubted that they had been listened to!

Becoming a great listener is a skill we can learn and, when we apply it, will help our children feel loved and respected. So let's break down some specific ways we can develop and strengthen the skill of listening.

SHOW INTEREST

Have you ever had something important to say to someone who seemed to be focused on everything *but* you? Maybe she was pulling out her phone, glancing at her watch, looking disinterested, or even changing the subject. How did that make you feel? Did you get the impression that she wasn't interested in you or that what you had to say wasn't important?

The body language we use when interacting with others is very important. The game of charades is a word guessing game but relies heavily on the body through expressions, movements, and signals that provide other players with the nonverbal feedback they need to guess the correct answer. Organizations that work with kids tap into aspects of this game as an aid to increase children's awareness of how emotions and feelings can be communicated through facial expressions and body language.

Through body language, we can offer our kids reinforcement, encouragement, and affirmation that their thoughts are valued and respected (whether or not we agree with them on every point).

Are you constantly multitasking while your children are talking to you? Whether we're looking at the computer or phone, or even focusing on essentials like housework or cooking, if we aren't giving them undivided attention, our kids might decide that we don't care about what they're saying. Worse, they could come away with the feeling that, deep down, they are not important enough to be heard.

Ultimately, this can affect our children's developing self-esteem. So it is critically important that we keep the channels open by showing them that we are listening. They need to get the message that what is important to them is important to us. Listening actively also helps build trust. If we don't encourage them to communicate with us regularly, then when they are in distress (and really need our input), how likely will they be to approach us for help?

So how can we use our body language to show our children that we are interested in what they have to say? What nonverbal cues are we sending? Are they positive or negative, affirming or critical, welcoming or discouraging? Here's what we can do to set the right tone:

- *Stop what we're doing and look them in the eyes.* This is often difficult when our hands are full of laundry or dirty dishes or we have an important deadline. Naturally, there will be times we cannot just stop. But when we can, even if it's not convenient, it is important to look them right in the eyes.

- *Signal that we're listening.* This happens nonverbally, like nodding our head or physically touching them.

- *Say it back.* The best way to show our kids we are listening is to repeat back what we heard them say.

There will be moments when we cannot give children our undivided attention. There will be times when we are buried by something (maybe literally by laundry) and they want us to stop and hear in full detail what happened at school or on the playground. At those times, we can stop for a moment, tell them that we want to hear what they have to say, then give them a specific time that we will give them our undivided attention—something like, "Let me finish what I am working on now, but I do want to hear the story of what happened. How about if we talk during dinner?"

LET THEM TALK

Have you ever had a conversation with someone who wouldn't let you finish a sentence? Maybe he was constantly interrupting and interjecting his opinion. Did you feel frustrated? Annoyed? How likely were you to want to continue talking or to have further conversations with that person?

If we constantly cut off our children, talk over them, tell them how to feel, and finish their sentences, they will get frustrated, too, and build the same resistance to having conversations with us.

Most of us would admit that we do this with our kids at least some of the time, hurrying them to get to the point so we can get on with whatever we need to do. But our attention and focus are more valuable than you might think—they are food for our children's souls.

How can we start signaling to our kids that it's safe to talk and that we want to hear what they have to say?

Try This! BETTER LISTENING

Benjamin Disraeli said, "Nature has given us two ears but only one mouth." To demonstrate how hard it is to listen and pay attention while someone else is talking or interrupting, have your child sing a familiar song out loud—make it a familiar Jewish song if you'd like, such as Adon Olam or, if it's around Passover, the Four Questions—while you read (out loud) a passage from a book. Can he get all the way through without making a mistake? Now, ask your child a few questions about what you were reading. Does he remember anything? Switch places so he can see how this works as well.

- *Listen carefully and respectfully* and give kids the opportunity to say everything they want to.

- *Give your undivided attention and maintain eye contact.* That way, even if they pause for a moment, they will feel comfortable continuing on if they have more to say.

- *Wait to ask questions or give opinions.* It can be tempting to jump in too soon, especially if children are having trouble articulating their emotions. It's OK to ask your kids, "Is there anything else you would like to say about this?" before you respond.

What's most important in this moment is that our kids are heard and understood. This is how we can get the best insight into what's going on inside their heads and hearts.

Look for Nonverbal Clues

As we mentioned above, nonverbal communication is crucial. Our kids' body language can give us important nonverbal clues to their emotional state. It can help us identify the intentions (feelings, emotions, frustrations) beyond the actual words being spoken. Here are some signs to watch out for:

- Tightened jaw or lips tensed

- "Micro-expressions" that are fleeting and involuntary giveaways

- Flat or excited tone of voice

- Nervous fidgeting

- Shoulder shrugging

- Clenched fists

- No eye contact

When children's body language demonstrates a strong emotion (like frustration, anger, or sadness), it is fine to address it. Try saying something like, "You look like you might be frustrated; tell me why." Or "Does this [fill in the blank] make you sad?" But keep it simple and open-ended so they feel comfortable continuing to talk.

KEEPING COOL

One of the biggest challenges in parenting is to control our emotions in the heat of the moment. When a child is yelling, acting out, or having a meltdown, how can we stay cool and not overreact ourselves?

One ancient Jewish precept from *Pirkei Avot* (*Ethics of the Fathers*), a collection of ancient Jewish wisdom, teaches us the definition of true strength: "Who is strong? One who has self-control" (4:1). There's no magic formula that can turn us into perfect parents every time, but with just a few principles and strategies, we can help practice this type of self-control:

- *Respond, don't react.* Reacting is matching an emotionally charged behavior with your own emotionally charged comeback. Responding is getting your emotions under control and thinking through the best way to resolve the situation. Don't ignore your emotions, just filter them so you can respond effectively. This creates a safe environment, where you're not belittling, imposing guilt, or criticizing.

- *Model self-control.* There will be times that we do lose our cool, and then we need to admit our lack of self-control to our kids and explain how we will work to do better.

- *Beware of overidentifying.* It's tempting to make our children's experiences our own, especially if we feel like they have been slighted or treated unfairly. While we do need to nurture and protect them, overidentifying can create unhealthy boundaries and give children the message that they can't deal with problems on their own.

Keeping our cool is a continuous process, because kids can flip that switch from calm to chaos at any time.

Staying levelheaded tells our kids that we are confident in their ultimate success. This message becomes even more crucial as they grow more independent. Our primary goal is to listen and understand so that we can help them navigate their own problems and concerns.

UNDERSTAND AND ARTICULATE THEIR FEELINGS

If we're listening by showing interest, letting our kids talk, watching their body language, and keeping cool, is that enough? Not quite. They may also need help putting their emotions into words. Being able to articulate emotions and feelings will benefit your children their whole lives.

What does articulating feelings mean? It includes being able to recognize emotions and verbalize them, building a vocabulary to communicate what's going on inside. Many children lack the emotional maturity to put emotions into words. Breaking this process down into steps can help us help our children to express themselves clearly.

- *First listen.* Don't minimize how your child feels. If your child's team has just lost a big game, saying, "I bet this is very disappointing for you" is much more helpful than "Let it go" or "Don't worry, you'll win the next one." The first statement validates his feelings and lets the child feel the disappointment; the others discount these normal feelings.

- *Don't pass judgment.* Sometimes, an emotional eruption seems ridiculous and tests our patience. "What does it matter if you don't have the exact right crayon color?" "Will having that exact Matchbox car *really* make or break your entire day?" But if it is important to our children, we need to listen and express our understanding. We won't always agree, but we need to be a safe sounding board.

- *Don't make assumptions about children's feelings.* Asking questions like "How do you feel about it?" or "What don't you like?" or "What's bugging you?" can open discussion more effectively than making statements like "Don't be angry" or "I know you're mad." It's easier to talk through problems if your child isn't keeping up a wall of defense.

- *Follow up general questions with more specific questions, based on your child's response.* Reflecting on what you're hearing will help your child line up her thoughts with what she's feeling inside. Use words that allow room for your child to disagree or clarify, like "seems" or "perhaps." Let children talk freely, using their own expressions.

- *Don't automatically give in to your child's feelings.* The goal is not to always protect children from disappointment or make sure they're constantly feeling happy and positive. There will be many times children are disappointed, don't think we're fair, or even cry and tell us how mean we are (or worse). That's okay. Avoid the temptation to fix the situation just to make them feel better. When we move in to fix whatever has happened, we take away the validity of their feelings because we take them as our own. We also lose the opportunity to help them articulate and address their own emotions and create a constructive plan in response.

A Yiddish proverb says, "No one is as deaf as the person who will not listen." Self-control and communication, constructive thinking, and emotional intelligence are skills we can cultivate to help our children get touch with their feelings and express them both accurately and productively. We need to make sure that we model this behavior and deliberately give our children the skills they need.

As we said above, respectful listening doesn't mean we'll always agree. That's why it's important to prioritize and hold fast to your family principles or religious traditions. Healthy emotional communication is important, but when there is a conflict between a child's feelings and a family's heritage, traditions, and guiding principles (like when a child wants to go to a football game instead of having family Shabbat dinner), healthy communication might involve acknowledging your children's feelings but reminding them that you're prepared to stand up for these larger values.

Communicate Respectfully

Traditionally, a challah cover is placed over the challah when the table is set for Shabbat. One explanation for this custom is that we don't want the challah to be embarrassed that it is blessed last, so we cover it up. One Shabbat, a family had a guest in their home for dinner. As they sat down at the table, the father realized that the children had forgotten to cover the challah and scolded them in front of the guest. To which the guest responded, "Sir, if we cover the challah so that it will not be embarrassed, then how much more so should we not embarrass a person."

It is so easy to get wrapped up in the duties and responsibilities of parenting that we often forget how we sound to our children. The tone we use to communicate at home sets the dynamic within the family: combative or peaceful, negative or positive, critical or affirming, mundane or joyful.

Jewish tradition emphasizes *derech eretz*, literally "the way of the land." This means that treating others with respect is simply what's expected of us. We demonstrate manners, decency, and proper behavior to each other.

Helping our children learn derech eretz, common decency and appropriate behavior, is a crucial but very difficult aspect of parenting. Saying "please" and "thank you," talking politely, and treating other people's property and feelings with respect should be our normal response, both inside and outside the home. But for this to happen, we need to teach and model this behavior.

Let's think through some ways we may or may not be modeling derech eretz in our own homes now.

Try This! LISTENING RESPECTFULLY

Games are a great way to get family members talking, rather than bickering, about things that really matter or about light topics. The game Apples to Apples even has a Jewish edition, which can be fun at the Shabbat table. Though recommended for players ages twelve and up, even younger children can join a parent's team. Players take turns judging which suggested word or phrase is closest to a given idea. For instance, which is most "refreshing"—the moon, "mazel tov," Elijah the Prophet, or Pharaoh? Finding connections between seemingly unrelated thoughts lets kids share their ideas in a respectful forum ("I think mazel tov is most refreshing because you can shout it anywhere, anytime!"). There are no right or wrong answers! This is all about having a chance to make kids' opinions count.

- Do we greet each other in a sincere and caring way when we get back together after having been apart?

- Do we say "please" and "thank you" when talking to each other?

- How do we handle frustration?

- Is what we do at home different from what we do outside of the home, when others are watching us?

- Do we treat family members with less consideration than we treat others?

The words we use every day with our children have the power to injure, to lift up, to tear down, to motivate, or to disappoint... and this can happen regardless of our intention.

We might not mean to make our children feel small or unimportant, but the words and tone we use in everyday dialogue might just be having that effect. Negative words create a critical and disapproving environment. Children are very sensitive; they notice how we talk to one another, especially at home. Effective communication requires courtesy, respect, consideration, and listening, and of course, discussion.

Express Anger Constructively

Here's a common scenario: you come home from work after an exhausting day to a house that looks like it's been hit by a tornado. You walk through the door and immediately start tripping over your children's jackets, backpacks, and toys, which have been strewn all over the floor. You're so tired that you have no patience to deal with this, not to mention the fact that you worked your tail off the previous day getting the house in order.

How do you think you might react?

- Sarcasm—"What do you think I am, the maid?"

- Insults—"You are the biggest slobs I have ever seen."

- Threats—"If you don't clean this up right now, you're grounded."

- Punishment—"Look at this house; you can't have any friends over for a month!"

- Revenge—"You didn't help me, so why should I help you?"

- The silent treatment—"Just don't talk to me for the rest of the day."

Will any of these reactions make the house cleaner or your family more peaceful and loving?

Derech eretz will never materialize if the way we speak at home is full of verbal jabs and stabs. Sarcasm and insults can create deep wounds; threats and punishments are pointless unless you follow through and enforce them; and the silent treatment only makes things more tense for everyone. Plus, none of these make things better going forward.

There are three basic ways we can deal with our own anger. We can explode, which usually leaves everyone feeling bad and doesn't fix the problem; we can remain upset but push it down and dwell on it inside, which often leads to a bigger outburst later; or we can express our feelings in a constructive way to actually resolve the situation.

Anger isn't always a negative thing. The Bible contains several examples of righteous anger, like Queen Esther's response when she learns of Haman's plot to destroy the Jewish people, risking her life to tell the king so he would stop Haman.

While anger is normal, it is powerful. It is like a buzz saw—used improperly, it can cause tremendous harm and pain. So Judaism teaches that there is a time, place, and correct way of demonstrating anger, especially in the face of evil. Just think of how the civil rights movement channeled anger constructively to transform society.

A peaceful home is not a place where no one ever gets angry. It is important for our children to know that anger can be healthy and normal. But it's what we do with that anger that counts. In a peaceful home, anger is expressed in a safe and constructive way. As we read in Proverbs 15:18, "A hot-tempered man stirs up strife, but he who is slow to anger quiets contention." Uncontrolled parental anger is like fanning the flames of a fire. As you are able to reduce your anger, you will see your children's anger diminish. It's not as simple as an off switch, so be patient and realistic. But as surely as removing oxygen gradually extinguishes a flame, slowing your own anger will quiet it in your children.

Think of someone blowing up a balloon: blowing and blowing until it bursts. Then think of someone blowing up a balloon until it's large but not at the breaking point. Visualize slowly letting the air out of this balloon in front of a pinwheel. What happens? The energy in the balloon moves the pinwheel. By not letting ourselves reach the bursting point, we can harness our anger, let out our feelings slowly, and express them constructively.

Articles, news feeds, and blogs are full of stories of the damage done to families and individuals as a result of persistent and unresolved anger. Over and over, learning specific details of a tragedy, we hear of anger that had been simmering until it boiled over. The other, and more common, occurrence is sudden anger. When this happens, a person's behavior is taken over by rapid, aggressive, exploding rage toward another person. Directly and indirectly, we have seen and experienced how this kind of anger can damage relationships.

Long before it became one of psychology's hot topics, Jewish scholars recognized that unchanneled anger was an enormous danger on both a personal and a societal level. Jewish tradition records this phenomenon in the Talmud by saying: "When a wise man loses his temper, he loses his wisdom" (Talmud, *Pesachim* 66b). When our judgment is clouded by strong negative emotion, rational thinking is diminished, and the result is conflict.

Parental rage can have a terrifying effect on children. But parenting brings its own unique challenges to anger management. It's natural to ask ourselves, "How can we keep a cap on our anger when we are dealing with the frustrations, challenges, and tests of our patience that naturally come with raising children?" Even best-selling parenting author Nancy Samalin has said, "I never knew I could be so angry until I was a parent." It can be frustrating to see our idealism, as parents, dissolve into the frustrating realities of daily life.

Combining the wisdom of Jewish tradition with current parenting knowledge, we can deal with anger in ways that will positively influence our children and bring harmony to the whole family. The advantages of learning to express our anger constructively are profound: we will teach our children to respond to anger in a healthy way, we will enjoy internal peace, and shalom bayit will be reinforced in a home less fractured by stress.

ANGER CAN BE A "RUG"

Saying "I'm angry" is actually a catch-all that hides many other emotions. The word *anger* lies like a rug on top of, and sometimes covering, other strong feelings. Below the surface lie deeper emotions, not as easy to identify or articulate.

When our kids dump a box of Lego bricks over a freshly cleaned floor or we come home to a sink full of dirty dishes, are we only angry, or are we perhaps also frustrated or simply exhausted?

When older kids come home past curfew, are we simply angry, or could our emotions be fueled by worry, disappointment, or insecurity over not being in control?

How about when our children act up in front of other people? Could our anger over that behavior be hiding our embarrassment over how we might be perceived as parents?

What parenting situations make you angry every single time they happen?

Using anger as a rug to cover our true emotions doesn't only apply to parenting. When a friend forgets our birthday or a scheduled lunch, our anger could be covering up a deeper sadness or hurt feelings.

Our homes will never be truly peaceful if there are negative emotions lying beneath the surface. If our actual feelings are consistently covered up by anger, then we can never truthfully deal with the root of the conflict. To create and maintain a peaceful home and have any hope of shalom bayit, we can lift up the "rugs" and put our true emotions into words, learning how to honestly communicate what is at the core, the heart, of our feelings. Dealing with these deeper emotions is the key to overcoming and resolving them.

How can we pull up the rug that is covering our true feelings? Follow these three basic steps:

Step 1. Recognize when you start to feel angry

Watch for your body's physical signals when anger starts to kick in. These reactions can serve as good indicators to us that we may be close to losing control—reactions like a flushed face, sweating, heart beating a mile a minute, feeling close to tears, shaking, clenched or grinding teeth.

These signs differ from person to person, but most people are able to recognize at least one physical effect of anger. By recognizing your body's response to it, you can start figuring out how to keep anger in check and not let it escalate too quickly or beyond control.

Step 2: Collect yourself

The Book of Proverbs teaches us, "One who is slow to anger is better than the mighty, and one whose temper is controlled [is better] than one who captures a city" (Proverbs 16:32).

Because anger can explode into outbursts of rage that leave us full of regret, we need an intentional, advance plan to keep our bodies and emotions under control. Think through what steps might help you calm down. For example: stop and take deep breaths, count backward from ten, do something distracting (squeeze a stress ball, doodle, clean the countertop), or put on soothing music. Sometimes, getting control of our emotions requires taking a little break in another room (kind of like a parent's time-out).

Once the intense feeling of anger has lessened a bit, we can go back and talk things through. The main objective is to calm down before dealing with the problem. The idea that a strong emotional issue has to be dealt with immediately is a myth. As the verse from Proverbs above shows, Judaism teaches that it's best to step back first.

Step 3: Put feelings into words

Once our emotions are under control, we will have more clarity about our deeper feelings and be better able to reasonably put those feelings into words. How we talk to our children creates the foundation for our influence on them. Will they actually listen to us, value what we are saying, and apply it to their behavior?

Once we learn to pinpoint our real feelings and express them constructively, we can deal with the issue(s) that led to the conflict in the first place. That is why identifying feelings and appropriately expressing them are essential elements of good communication: they help us get past the roadblock of our strong emotional responses.

There will be times when expressing our feelings in a healthy way is enough to keep peace at home. At other times, we'll need to work through a legitimate problem that is causing the conflict, such as sibling rivalry.

Minimize Sibling Rivalry

One day, Sarah and David's father brought home two cupcakes from the bakery, one chocolate and one vanilla. To be fair, Dad had the children each pick a number between one and ten, and told them that the number closest to the one he'd written down and hidden in his pocket would win. Sarah picked five and David two. The number in Dad's pocket was six, so Sarah won. "Okay, Sarah," said Dad. "You get to choose first." Sarah responded, "No, I want to wait and see which one David chooses. That's the one I want!"

Sibling rivalry has been around since Cain killed Abel out of jealousy and anger. And that is the root of sibling rivalry: competition and struggle to come out on top; the drive to be the best, to get the most, to be the favorite.

Sibling rivalry begins very early as little ones compete for their parents' affection. In the Torah, Abraham favored Isaac over Ishmael. Isaac's sons Jacob and Esau began struggling inside their mother Rebekah's womb; when the twins were grown, Rebekah encouraged Jacob to trick his father into giving him the birthright. Imagine how Jacob's son Joseph, with his coat of many colors, must have annoyed his brothers to push them to the point of almost killing him, then settling for "only" selling him into slavery, and lying to their grieving father? As the Book of Proverbs says, "A brother offended is harder to be won than a strong city" (Proverbs 18:19).

Any time people of different ages, personalities, temperaments, and interests live together, there is bound to be friction. The first step to minimizing sibling rivalry is to realize that this competition is natural and most likely will continue throughout our kids' childhoods. Even if we could do everything exactly right, we can't always control all the expressions or perceptions of favoritism. The biblical stories above remind us to actively work to keep the competition to a minimum, because if rivalry is allowed to go unchecked, not only will the idea of a peaceful home be a remote fantasy, but rampant rivalry will do real damage to children psychologically and harm their relationships with each other for the rest of their lives.

What lessons do you think we can learn from all the stories of sibling rivalry in the Torah?

Let's look in detail at how to respond to two common issues that can spark feelings of competition and animosity in our children: favoritism (real or perceived) and fighting.

Putting yourself in your children's shoes can help you refocus on what's really happening when sibling rivalry seems out of control.

Four-year-old Oren got into a tussle with his two-year-old brother, Ari. As they both grabbed at the same toy car, Ari suddenly fell backward and banged his head. He ran to his mother screaming. When she saw a huge bump on Ari's head, she scolded Oren. Oren was upset and headed to the front door to try to leave. Just then, a light bulb went off in his mother's head and she said, "Oren, both of you were fighting. It's not only your fault that Ari got hurt." Almost immediately, Oren turned away from the door and went to get his doctor's bag to help his little brother feel better.

As Oren and Ari's mom discovered, taking a minute to figure out what our kids are thinking can quickly defuse a volatile situation. As soon as Oren wasn't worried that he was in trouble, he could react with compassion toward his brother.

RESPONDING TO FAVORITISM

"You like him/her better than me!"

In a perfect world, our children would never feel this way. But there will be plenty of times when it might seem like we favor one child over another or when we might come down harder on one child than another. Our children have their own personalities, interests, and temperaments, and we might even gravitate toward the child most similar to us. This doesn't necessarily mean our love is any stronger, but often our body language or actions might inaccurately convey that message to our other children.

Many elements factor into our children's feelings about themselves and each other. Kids are sometimes jealous of siblings for things beyond our control, like talent in sports or academics. If one child has a disability, that child may get so much more attention that other children feel slighted or less important. Our kids may also be picking up on inadvertent signals, like laughing at one child's jokes more, bragging about one child's accomplishments, or giving the majority of our attention to the most demanding child.

By listening to our children and watching their body language, we can detect signs of jealousy or resentfulness, like bullying, teasing, mocking, making fun, or constantly demanding our attention. When these signals appear, it's time to examine the possibility that we could be showing favoritism to one child over another. Sometimes, fixing the problem can be as simple as acknowledging the slighted child's feelings and praising his or her talents and strengths. Or it may take a little more effort, like setting aside some special time to spend only with that child.

RESPONDING TO SIBLING FIGHTING

"It's mine!" "No, it's mine. I got it first!"

Our children's fighting can drive us crazy, especially if it's constant bickering over toys, clothes, books, or anything else. Always having to mediate between kids can really get on a parent's nerves. Here are some ideas for minimizing fights over little issues like material possessions:

- *Be very clear about which things (toys, clothes, books) belong to which child* and which are "family possessions" that any child can use. Label these things if necessary.

- *Establish a procedure for borrowing someone else's stuff.* Do children always have to ask permission? What if the child who owns it isn't home? Can the parents then give another child permission to borrow it?

- *Establish a process beforehand* to deal with what happens if someone's item gets broken or ruined while in the possession of another child. As a matter of respect, an item should be returned in the same condition as when it was lent.

- *Be sure that we as parents also respect the rules* for borrowing things from our kids.

How we respond to our children's disputes can either intensify or lessen them. It can be tempting to us, as parents, to jump all over the child who seems to be at fault, but often this only triggers more tension and rivalry.

Imagine your kids are in another room and something happens to disrupt the peace. You hear yelling and walk in to find them hitting each other. What should you do?

Rather than play detective, make the clear point that hitting is never okay, regardless of the wrong that was committed. Instead, your children can choose to walk away, come tell you, or figure out something else to do. Then, you can facilitate a discussion between the kids to solve the problem and make sure it does not happen again.

If we can keep a cool head and stay calm (often easier said than done), we can help resolve the situation without adding fuel to the fire.

Here are some more ideas that can help prevent problems between our kids or head them off before they escalate:

- *Set basic guidelines for your kids*, clarifying acceptable and unacceptable behavior.

- *Embrace each child as an individual,* and celebrate his or her unique qualities and special accomplishments.

- *Avoid comparing children to each other,* which can make them feel hurt or insecure.

- *Praise your kids often* for treating each other with respect and courtesy.

- *Don't take sides;* encourage children to settle their own differences if they're old enough to do this without resorting to physical violence.

- *Listen to your children* and let them privately vent their frustrations about each other. Then acknowledge that their feelings are a normal part of growing up.

- *Show your children that what is important to them is important to you.* You can do this by spending time with them individually and doing something that they are specifically interested in.

- *Address blatant favoritism* with family members (especially grandparents), close friends, teachers, and others, as needed. It's difficult to confront family members (especially when the behavior is not intentional), but when it's harmful to your children, it needs to be addressed.

THE BENEFITS OF SIBLINGS

Let's not forget that sibling relationships are not all about competition and rivalry. There is so much value in having brothers and sisters as allies and friends within our families, sharing similar traditions and experiences. If these relationships are steered and guided in a healthy, constructive way during childhood, hopefully they will provide good friendships and support into adulthood.

That said, natural rivalry does have benefits. With their siblings, children learn in the safe setting of home how to assert themselves, protect themselves, deal with not getting their own way, and resolve conflicts. These are very important life skills. Children also learn that fights can be short-lived and that soon enough they'll make up and be friends again.

Sibling rivalry also teaches the priceless gift of loyalty. Think about the reconciliation of Joseph and his brothers in Egypt; after years of strife, they were able to stand together again, as a family. Our kids will receive the immeasurable and precious opportunity to root for each other, to be in one another's corner, and to feel joy for their siblings' successes.

Wrap-Up

Of course, there are more challenges to parenting than just keeping a peaceful home, and we have a lot more to cover in the chapters ahead.

But as we wrap up this chapter dealing with communicating, listening, feelings, problem solving, and sibling rivalry, let's end with a beautiful Jewish blessing. On Shabbat evening, we traditionally bless our sons to be like Joseph's sons Ephraim and Manasseh, two brothers who lived in peaceful harmony. Just before their grandfather Jacob died, he called his grandsons in and said, "In time to come, the people of Israel will use you as a blessing. They will say, 'May God make you like Ephraim and Manasseh'" (Genesis 48:20).

Why did Jacob choose to bless Ephraim and Manasseh? Because, Jewish tradition teaches, they were the first brothers mentioned in the Bible who did not fight with each other; they were friends known for their good deeds.

Over the years, a parallel blessing has been created for daughters, wishing them the strength of the matriarchs Sarah, Rebekah, Rachel, and Leah.

For a boy:
May God make you like Ephraim and Manasseh.
Y'simcha Elohim k'Efrayim v'chiM'nasheh.

For a girl:
May God make you like Sarah, Rebekah, Rachel, and Leah.
Y'simeich Elohim k'Sarah, k'Rivkah, k'Rachel uch'Leah.

For all children:
May God bless you and protect you.
May God's face shine toward you and show you favor.
May God look favorably upon you and grant you peace.

Y'varech'cha Adonai v'yishm'recha.
Ya'er Adonai panav eilecha vichuneka.
Yisa Adonai panav eilecha v'yaseim l'cha shalom.

What parents wouldn't want to bless their children in the name of shalom bayit, a peaceful home, and peace between their children?

From oy to Joy!

You'll know that you are moving from oy to joy when your child...

- takes extra time to prepare a healthy snack for his younger brother.

- waits until you finish what you're saying before telling you excitedly about her new gym routine.

- expresses anger in words, without hitting or slamming doors.

- does not argue when you ask him to participate in a family meeting.

chapter 2

Establish Routines

"Parents who establish routines and incorporate rituals
into their children's lives are providing them with an invaluable
foundation and tools for living a full, rich life."
—*Caron Blau Rothstein, Jewish educator*

"Rhythms establish a foundation of cooperation and connection."
—*Kim John Payne, M.Ed.,* Simplicity Parenting: Using the Extraordinary
Power of Less to Raise Calmer, Happier, and More Secure Kids

■ ■ ■

*The dramatic stories of the Bible have a lot to teach us, even when
their subjects are behaving poorly. When the Israelites left Egypt,
they were excited and spiritually charged by all the miracles, the
marvelous plagues, and the wondrous occurrences that led to
their freedom. But when they reached Mount Sinai and Moses
left them to receive the Torah, he was delayed, and the people
began to panic. Without his leadership and guiding hand, their*

faith faltered. They complained to Aaron, his brother, "This man, Moses, who led us out of Egypt, we don't know what has become of him" (Exodus 32:1). By calling him a "man," they're pointing out that he's mortal—that anything could have happened on the mountain, and that perhaps he's never coming back. The story reminds us of how delays and changes in routine can leave us feeling vulnerable and afraid. Stripped of their routines, the Children of Israel rushed to recreate something familiar from their time in Egypt: an idol, the golden calf.

■ ■ ■

Imagine a school with no routines—no established start time, dismissal time, lunchtime, periods, not even policies or syllabi. How well would that go? How effective would the teaching be if children were just randomly coming in and out of the classroom? Kids wouldn't know when they would eat lunch or when they could use the bathroom. How would they feel? How would we feel in their position? Irritable? Annoyed? Anxious?

Routines give us security, a sense of inner peace. No matter what else happens, we know we can rely on some things remaining constant. Jewish life has been strengthened and reinforced throughout history by traditions, customs, and routines, the glue that has held Jewish families and communities together. Adding simple practices to our everyday lives is reassuring to children, especially in our fast-moving culture. Routines will make them more calm, secure, productive, and resistant to negative influences. They will also provide bound-aries and a kind of a protective shield around our children and their emotions, like a filter through which they can process all the information coming at them.

Ultimately, routines are about how we use our time. So in this chapter, we focus on three ways to make the flow of time in our families better. Our ancestors knew this, and in the hectic lives so many of us lead, it's more valuable than ever that we use time to get things done, reduce our stress, and bring our immedi-ate and extended families closer together. Jewish traditions give us guidance about how we can:

- Create predictability

- Sanctify the passage of time through Shabbat

- Establish memorable traditions

Create Predictability

Not knowing what to expect can exert a powerful effect on stress levels and insecurity in people of all ages, but the effect it has on children can be much more dramatic. A school with no schedule, rules, or predictability can't educate children. This is also true at home, with even more far-reaching effects. Children living in homes with few routines or boundaries can develop a deep-rooted insecurity that will inhibit their ability to focus, discipline them-selves, or control their emotions.

Children need to feel confident that someone is in control of their world and that they will be taken care of and protected, no matter what. As parents, we can't control the outside world, but we do have a say in what happens at home. If we create an environment where children know they can rely on us and where they're confident their needs will be met, we can free their minds from fear and confusion that could work against healthy development.

SCHEDULES AND ROUTINES

An understanding of the importance of order and predictability is woven throughout Jewish teachings. Shabbat comes every week, holidays are celebrated year after year, we have set times for prayers, and special ceremonies mark life-cycle events.

Every parent of a newborn knows how important a schedule is to the stability of a home. Newborns don't know day from night or when to sleep. So we work to get our babies on a schedule, to teach them what to do and when to do it. Once the baby is on a schedule, the peace and stability of the entire house improves.

A schedule offers children consistency and helps them feel secure that their needs will be met on a regular basis. It reduces worry and anxiety, which in turn creates a calmer, more peaceful environment. But we're not talking about a rigid, inflexible, unrealistic structure. A basic, consistent schedule that your child can rely on will build her trust and security. And it's a myth that only younger children need this type of structure. In our busy world, all children, even teenagers, need to feel secure and have predictability in their lives.

Creating predictability as children get older also helps eliminate nagging and renegotiating rules, which is exhausting, frustrating, and probably not very effective anyway. Nagging and renegotiating usually manage to restore peace only until the next time we have to negotiate a meal or bedtime, at which point the whole process begins again.

What schedules and routines have you found helpful in your family?

Have you ever heard one of these lines from your kids? "I don't want to go to bed yet." "I'm not tired." "It's too early." "I'm not ready to eat." "My show isn't over." "It's not fair." Creating a schedule around essential functions—eating, sleeping, homework, television/computer time—leaves less room for argument and negotiation. Children who feel secure in these set times will realize that it's a waste of time to try fight. This will make them calmer and our homes more peaceful.

We can keep in mind that what we are instilling in our children now will serve them (either positively or negatively) in the future. Integrating routines into everyday family life will teach our kids how to structure their own lives and homes (someday) in a way that adds security, calmness, and peace. The advice columnist Ann Landers, daughter of Russian Jewish immigrants, wrote, "In the final analysis it is not what you do for your children but what you have taught them to do for themselves that will make them successful human beings."

Let's look at some intentional practices that will make our daily activities run more smoothly and give kids the structure they need.

Starting the Day (getting up)

- *Allow enough time to get off to a good start,* especially when kids are getting ready for school. Aside from the necessities (using the bathroom, brushing teeth, eating breakfast), children need enough time for their minds to wake up to the day ahead. Stress is tougher to deal with in the morning, and a constant state of panic only adds to the tension.

- *Do things in the same order each day.* This lets children know what to expect, so there's less chaos and negotiating.

Try This! A PEACEFUL START TO THE DAY

Set kid-friendly morning blessings to easy, catchy little tunes, to give the morning a fun but meaningful start. Modeh Ani is a prayer in which we give thanks for waking. There's a fun, contemporary version on the CD *Oy Baby! 2,* along with a number of other Jewish songs in English and simple Hebrew that you can sing every day and on special occasions. Ease into making this a part of your routine, introducing songs during transition times, such as when kids are sitting down for breakfast, waiting for the bus, or riding to school. You'd be surprised how much listening to music during these times helps add predictability and peace to the start of the day—along with smiling, humming, and toe tapping!

Your family's order might include: get out of bed, get dressed, make the bed, eat breakfast, brush teeth and hair. Practiced consistently, this lets kids know what is supposed to happen next.

- *Set standards for extras like electronics.* If these are allowed in the morning, it should happen only after every necessary item on the schedule is completed.

After-School/Social Activities

- *Be realistic.* Every child cannot participate in every activity. It is unsustainable to take multiple children to multiple activities every day. More importantly, children need unstructured time to decompress and relax.

- *Help kids prioritize.* What's most important: Sports? Dance? An instrument? Often, listing extra activities in order of importance helps kids understand why they can't do everything and highlights what is most important.

- *Plan ahead.* Make a family calendar listing everyone's activities. Start with nonnegotiable items, like school requirements and medical appointments. Then fill in sports, social, and extracurricular activities. This visual aid helps older kids understand the bigger picture of the family schedule.

- *Set firm boundaries.* Establish crystal-clear expectations of "nonnegotiables": what children are allowed to do and with whom, curfew, consequences, etc. Boundaries will change as kids get older. But they apply as soon as children can start doing things on their own.

- *Talk to your kids about building trust and earning privileges.* Explain how they can earn privileges and more independence and that when trust gets broken, privileges can be lost.

Mealtimes

- *Eat together.* It's that simple. Your meals don't have to be fancy, or pretty, or even all that peaceful. But the act of spending set time together can have a big impact on our children. Sit around the table and share highlights of each person's day. Try the game Roses and Thorns, in which each person takes a turn describing a good thing that happened that day (their "rose") and a low moment or tough problem he or she had to deal with (their "thorn"). It's a fun, easy way to identify the *oys* and highlight the daily joys of life.

- *Acknowledge the gifts of food and each other.* Offering a blessing or expression of thanks before and after eating can separate mealtime from the rest of our day. This works whether we are appreciating the skills of those who helped create the food, the Creator of all life, or both. Judaism offers traditional prayers and blessings for before and after meals that are straightforward and easy to implement. These reflections can deepen and enrich your family's life.

- *Create a spirit of cooperation around mealtime.* Get everyone to pitch in and help. Try creating an informal chart of basic tasks (like clearing the table) that clarifies responsibilities from day to day (based on your family's preference). Recognizing each person's contribution, accompanied by appreciative words, is often enough to reinforce these positive behaviors. Then, make time for family fun if you can.

Ending the Day

- *Allow enough time for children to wind down.* Establish the things that must be done (shower or bath, teeth brushed, toys put away) beforehand, then have a set time to start the pre-bedtime activities.

- *Set a bedtime.* Don't negotiate it. If it's lights-out at a certain time and your kids want to read for a little while, work that into the schedule so they are still getting the sleep they need.

- *Read together at bedtime.* This is an excellent way to connect and share the gift of imagination. Encouraging an older child to read to a younger child will benefit both. Books should be age appropriate but don't necessarily need to be short or simple. Reading one chapter a night is a great way to continue a dialogue with our kids and gives everyone something to look forward to at the end of each day. Set limits ahead of time so everyone knows when story time will end. For Jewish children, the PJ

Library program provides age-appropriate books at no cost that celebrate our traditions and heritage. Check out www.pjlibrary.org for more information.

- *Express gratitude.* Tell your children what you are thankful for each day, and encourage them to do the same. Can they name three positive moments or their top moment of the day? As we'll see in chapter seven, being thankful together and sharing our experiences can bond families and increase stability and shalom bayit as well.

- *Don't rush.* Give kids time to talk about their day, and listen carefully. As they open up a bit, try to dig a little deeper by asking questions to get more insight into their emotions. As we'll see, a safe environment is important to allow children to talk, which means not interrupting or "correcting" the way they feel. Reflecting like this can sometimes lead to deeper theological questions and be a valuable entry point to discussing our beliefs and values with kids.

When your family's schedules are organized, life flows more peacefully. But at times, spontaneity, perhaps as the result of last-minute changes, is also important. Spontaneous moments are part of the mystery and essence of life that fill us with feeling, hope, energy, and passion. They also help us become more flexible, adaptive, and resilient, putting aside structure to let loose and enjoy.

Through creating schedules and routines, no matter what is going on in the outside world, our children's most personal and intimate space (the home) can be that safe haven that they need to become strong and confident.

Keep in mind that there is no "perfect way" to do any of this. Personalize your routines to your family's needs, and keep them as consistent as you can. The objective is to bring security, stability, peace, and calm to your children and your lives.

Try This! ROUTINES TO END THE DAY

Use a calming, meaningful meditation, poem, or prayer. Judaism traditionally includes the Sh'ma in the bedtime routine. This short prayer, *Sh'ma Yisrael, Adonai Eloheinu, Adonai Echad,* means "Hear O Israel, Adonai is our God, Adonai is One." This prayer reminds us of our Jewish faith and connection with God. A few good children's books on the Sh'ma include *The Bedtime Sh'ma: A Good Night Book* and *Goodnight Sh'ma.* For older children (and for ourselves!), the Sh'ma can become a form of meditation, a way of focusing and relaxing mind and body at the end of the day. In his book *Jewish Meditation: A Practical Guide,* Rabbi Aryeh Kaplan writes that "the Torah itself prescribes that [the Sh'ma] be said twice daily, and it seems highly probable that this was originally prescribed as a short daily meditation for all of Israel." Try not to rush through your kids' Sh'ma—even if you're in a hurry to get on with your own evening.

Sanctify the Passage of Time through Shabbat

Along with daily schedules and routines, Judaism offers us the opportunity to sanctify a period of time every single week through celebrating Shabbat. Every week, this joyous tradition brings us together, refreshes us, and gives us something always to look forward to.

Having a reliable and secure time of peace, togetherness, and relaxation that stands out from the other days of the week is probably our most effective connection to Jewish continuity.

While the rest of our week may feel somewhat beyond our control, Shabbat puts us back in the driver's seat, carving out time in which we emphasize that our lives are about more than what we do in our jobs and at school and after-school activities. Reconnecting with this higher purpose is one of the most remarkable tools for families to maintain their religious identity and create a sense of security.

WHAT WE GAIN FROM SHABBAT

There is a well-known saying, "More than the Jews have kept the Sabbath, the Sabbath has kept the Jews." (Ahad Ha-Am) Setting aside one special day each week offers us connection, continuity, and security in who we are and where we've come from. Shabbat can also be the link between Jewish parenting and smart parenting. It's the foundation on which we build and nurture our families and our future.

On Shabbat, we don't just sit down to eat. We prepare. We make the meal unique. We have special food, special wine. We take our time. We reflect. We talk. We sing. We relax together. We connect with the beauty of our tradition. We bless our children. These exceptional moments can give our children something predictable to look forward to every week and also offer them an abundance of positive memories for life. These moments provide a sense of consistency, security, and belonging.

Could you add any special favorite foods to your family's Shabbat meal?

A child's sense of identity (and thus their self-esteem) develops early in life, and what goes on at home makes a deep early impression. Keep in mind that celebrating Shabbat does not need to be "all or nothing" and can be tailored to our own families and lives. The purpose is to connect us to each other and to our heritage.

MAKE THE ENTIRE DAY SPECIAL

The purpose of Shabbat is to take a break and focus on the blessings of what we have. We set aside one day— from sunset on Friday to sunset on Saturday—to enjoy our Jewish heritage and traditions. Hopefully, this is always a day our children cherish and in which they eagerly participate. For that to happen, Shabbat should feel special. Here are some traditional Jewish ideas that can be used in or adapted for your own home.

- *Light candles.* Light has connected the Jewish people for thousands of years. Every Friday at sundown, we welcome the respite that Shabbat brings by lighting candles and saying a blessing over them. We can reinforce shalom bayit by using candle lighting as a way to express gratitude for the blessings of our children and other family members. The symbolic light of Shabbat candles also reminds us to bring light into other people's lives and to recognize the good others have done for us. Lighting candles gives us not only a predictable and beautiful way to enter Shabbat, but also the added blessing of remembering what is good, what is important, and what we are thankful for.

- *Have a Shabbat meal together.* Earlier, we discussed the importance, both emotionally and socially, of regular mealtimes. Though getting together for mealtimes is not always possible on a weekday, Shabbat should be different. It arrives each Friday evening, whether we're ready for it or not. By the end of a hectic week of work, school, and other demands, we all need a break. Make the Shabbat meal feel different, unique, and valuable. We could do this with songs and blessings, special foods like challah (we've even given you a recipe at the end of this chapter) or an extra-special dessert, involving our children, or anything else that makes it feel out of the ordinary.

- *Keep it "doable."* Shabbat does not need to be a major production or become such an exhausting routine that there's no joy in it. That isn't sustainable, and it will not create the predictability and positive memories we want to instill. A Shabbat celebration looks very different for families with young children than it does for a family with teenagers. Do what works for you. If it's hard for young children to sit through an entire Shabbat meal, let them leave the table.

- *Give children ownership of the day* by letting them make some of the important decisions regarding food, activities, songs, etc. What would make it more meaningful for them? Let them help decide.

- *Be patient.* If Shabbat is new to your family, it will take time for you to feel comfortable and experience more joy than oy. Don't expect all the rewards immediately. Just keep offering your family the predictability, security, and togetherness that this day brings. If we prioritize Shabbat, eventually our kids will begin to feel more secure and treasure it, too.

- *Introduce a special Shabbat activity for Saturday afternoon*, like playing a board game or taking a walk together, or going to services on Saturday afternoon or evening for Havdalah to mark the close of Shabbat.

Shabbat is a privilege, a treasure, a journey. It offers us at least one moment, one meal, one day a week for intimate family connection. Each family member can understand who he or she is and the joy that family provides. Shabbat also produces a sense of

Try This! BAKE A CHALLAH FOR SHABBAT

A fun way to get your kids involved in and excited about Shabbat is to bake with them ahead of time. Here's a tried-and-true challah recipe to get you started!

Quick and Easy Challah

½ cup lukewarm water

1 tsp. sugar

2¼ tsp. active dry yeast
  or ⅔ ounce fresh yeast

½ cup canola oil

3 Tbsp. honey

3½–4 cups bread flour

1 tsp. salt

2 large eggs

1 egg yolk mixed with
  1 Tbsp. cold water

Poppy or sesame seeds, or
  other toppings, if desired

1. In a deep bowl, place water and sugar, then sprinkle in the yeast. (Be sure the water is only lukewarm; if it is too hot, it will kill the yeast, and the bread will not rise.) Let this mixture sit for 5 to 10 minutes until the yeast is dissolved.

2. After the yeast is dissolved, stir in canola oil and honey.

3. Beat in 1½ cups flour, add 1 tsp. salt, and beat again.

4. Add 2 eggs and beat well with a spoon.

5. Blend in an additional 1½ to 2 cups of flour, until you have a soft dough that isn't too sticky to knead (if it's clinging to your fingers when you touch it, add more flour). Turn out onto table or a flat surface.

6. To knead dough, make a flat circle, fold the top half over the bottom half, and push into it with the heels of your palms. Pull the dough like taffy, stretching it out and then folding it up. Turn dough a quarter-circle and repeat.

7. Knead the dough for about 5 minutes, adding a little more flour (up to about about ½ cup total) every time the dough starts to feel sticky.

8. Give the dough a final light kneading (1 minute), adding up to ¼ cup flour if the dough seems sticky.

9. Shape the dough into a ball. Cover with plastic wrap and let rise 45–90 minutes.

10. Cut the ball of dough into three equal portions, form these into strips, roll out and braid them. If you've never done this before, there are lots of how-to videos on YouTube. You can divide the dough to make more than one challah or form several smaller rolls by tying the strips into knots.

11. Place shaped challahs on a baking sheet lined with parchment paper. Cover with plastic wrap and let rise until doubled in size (approximately an hour and a half). It may take less time, so keep an eye on the dough so that it does not grow more than double in size.

12. Gently brush with the egg yolk mixed with water and sprinkle on poppy or sesame seeds, if desired, or let your kids invent a new favorite topping ("Everything" challah, anyone?). Bake at 375 degrees (400 for gas oven) until golden brown (approximately 20 minutes). Enjoy!

community with other Jews and lets our children feel connected to friends who are practicing the same thing.

By sharing Shabbat with our children, we let them know, in a way that goes beyond words, that there are some things more important than our own personal comfort zones (like singing out loud in front of people), while celebrating who we are and where we've come from.

Regardless of what may have happened during the prior six days, this seventh day is special and meant for us and for them. Our children will feel secure in how much we love and are blessed by them. And hopefully, we also will remind ourselves of the sacred responsibility, privilege, and joy of being a parent.

Establish Memorable Traditions

The annual cycle of Jewish holidays can also provide consistency and routine. It's easy to see how holidays contribute to our children's concepts of predictability. The holidays come in the same order, in the same season, every single year, offering many opportunities for families to get together and follow routines and rituals.

Like Shabbat, these special days let us slow down and step back from the hectic nature of everyday life to focus on our bigger priorities and goals, letting us remember our shared history. And just as we suggested with Shabbat, don't be afraid to put your own stamp on these special days to make them memorable occasions that your family will look forward to.

Each holiday marks an important date or event in our Jewish heritage. These traditions and customs have bonded the Jewish people together and are meant to be celebrated by individuals, with our families, and in our communities. Often, they become times for extended family members to gather, something that can too easily be put off because of our responsibilities and commitments. Observing these days also helps to secure and grow our children's character, identity, sense of belonging, and connection to their relatives.

Start creating your own traditions and practices around the holidays. For example:

- Use your grandmother's traditional Rosh Hashanah honey cake recipe, but make it into muffins instead of the traditional loaf (or pour some into a muffin-top pan for soft, delicious honey cake cookies).

- Build a sukkah with your kids, or buy a ready-made sukkah kit. It doesn't have to be perfect or elaborate. Imagine the fun your kids will have decorating it before the holiday, then sitting and eating inside.

- During Hanukkah, make up your own rules for a game of dreidel.

- Let kids toss marshmallows (representing the manna from heaven) around the seder table, to teach how food was provided in the desert.

- Create a Jewish "advent calendar," giving kids a small treat (it doesn't have to be food!) each day during the omer period, when we count the forty-nine days between Passover and Shavuot.

- Take a less familiar holiday, like Tu BiShevat, the "New Year of the Trees," and plan a fun new way to observe it with your kids. Invite friends to join in.

- Try creating a seder for a holiday other than Passover—perhaps around the many foods traditionally eaten on Rosh Hashanah...or what about Purim? Sukkot? What significant foods would your kids choose for these days, and why?

A wonderful example of a new Jewish tradition comes from Nina Beth Cardin and Gila Gevirtz, who mention in their book *Rediscovering the Jewish Holidays: Tradition in a Modern Voice* an initiative to create a new ritual object—a flag, which honors Esther of the Purim story and Jewish women throughout history. Yom Ha'atzma'ut (Israel Independence Day) is a traditional time for flag waving. Can your kids think of another special day for which they might want to design a flag?

Cardin and Gevirtz write, "Not only does each generation add its understanding and tradition to the treasury of Jewish life, but the diverse communities of the Jewish people also enrich Judaism."

Imagine inspiring such wonderful holiday memories for your children that, as adults, they'll be eager to bring their own children back to your house to celebrate, and in their own homes, they'll create their own versions of the traditions they cherished growing up. Talk about joy!

wrap-Up

The beloved musical *Fiddler on the Roof* provides a beautiful example of how Jewish routines helped offer strength in the face of adversity. Tevye, a man who is poor in the eyes of the world, feels great wealth in his family and their way of life. One of this musical's best-known songs is "Tradition." It praises the "quiet home" filled with daily prayers, with children who "mend and tend and fix."

This musical affirms how much our lives and beliefs are shaped by what we do on a regular basis. The things we do every day affect our shalom bayit. They will also provide our children with a secure foundation on which they will, one day, launch into their own lives. Let's do everything we can, today, to make their roots stable and strong, with traditions that can stand firm against any storm.

From oy to Joy!

You'll know that you are moving from oy to joy when your child...

- goes through his entire morning routine on his own.

- brushes her teeth before bedtime without being reminded.

- eagerly helps set the table for Shabbat.

- starts to look ahead to holidays and shares ideas for how to make celebrations special.

chapter 3

Foster Resilience

"I ask not for a lighter burden, but for broader shoulders."
—*Jewish proverb*

"The greatest glory in living lies not in never falling,
but in rising every time we fall."
—*Nelson Mandela*

■ ■ ■

We learn a lot about the importance of resilience from the biblical story of Jacob's son Joseph. Joseph was thrown into a pit by his brothers, sold into slavery, carried off to Egypt, falsely accused of a crime, and imprisoned. Imagine how devastated he must have felt! How easy would it have been for him to lose hope and give up?

Instead, Joseph turned his situation around using his gifts and talents. With his ability to interpret dreams, and his leadership and organizational skills, he not only worked his way out of prison but eventually became the second most powerful person in Egypt.

■ ■ ■

To most people, resilience means grit, what's traditionally known as courage, resolve, or strength of character. In our children's lives, resilience means being able to bounce back and to make the best of hardships and challenges. Being resilient doesn't mean going through life without pain and stress, nor does it mean overcoming everything that gets in the way. But resilient people have the tenacity to work through obstacles and succeed where many others might fail.

Many factors determine a person's grit; it's not something we simply inherit at birth. Resilience is developed and learned. Everyone has had bad experiences, suffered illness, lost friends and family, and endured problems in relationships or at work. In our kids' lives, most are familiar with the feeling of turning in a project and not getting the marks they expected, or of being picked last for a team. But there is a difference in how we respond to the tough moments of life. Do we keep a positive perspective and tackle life's issues head-on? Or do we fall apart when faced with obstacles and problems large and small?

In children, we often think of resilience in terms of their ability to cope with major disasters like death, divorce, and other life-changing events. But it is also a quality they'll use to handle life's little letdowns, like bullying at school, a teacher they don't get along with, or the failure to attain a goal they have been working toward, like the next color belt in Aikido or an audition for a music program.

Resilience can come from support systems like family and community, as well as from our traditions and beliefs.

We live in a stressful world. We cannot always protect our children and guarantee their safety and well-being against life's ups and downs. That's why teaching them resilience is important, so they can deal with uncertainties and challenges. It is also important for us to model resilience, because this makes it more likely that they will also successfully bounce back from the difficulties life throws their way.

Resilience involves both attitudes and behaviors, so it takes a combination of both to build this strength in children. When teaching resilience to our children, it is helpful to tap into both behavioral skills (like setting healthy limits and facing their own pain and disappointment) and emotional strengths (like the gifts of humor, optimism, and self-worth). These skills and strengths are like a protective shield that will keep the inevitable disappointments, failures, and hurts of life from penetrating so deeply that children become defeated or crushed. They enable all of us to successfully face life's challenges again and again.

In this chapter, we will explore four specific ways you can build resilience in your children:

- Set limits

- Let children experience disappointments

- Be positive

- Know how to laugh

The Book of Proverbs perhaps put it best: "A righteous man falls down seven times—and gets up" (Proverbs 24:16). Let's teach our kids how to keep on getting up whenever they fall down.

Set Limits

Imagine that you've heard about the most spectacular waterfall. Friends and travel guides have all told you that it's worth a great deal of physical effort to view it. So you set out, determined to see the waterfall. There are three possible paths you can take. The first one takes a lot of effort but gets you very close to your destination. However, when you arrive, a huge barrier blocks most of the view, with a sign prohibiting you from going any farther. Wouldn't that make you frustrated and annoyed? Would you be tempted to do something unwise, like climbing an unsafe barrier to make your trek worthwhile?

Instead, you attempt the second route, which has no obstructions and offers you a perfect and clear view of the raging, beautiful water. But the path is wet and slippery, and the slope where you have to stand to view it is dangerously steep. You're too preoccupied with the insecurity of the path to really enjoy the splendid view.

So you turn back and make one final effort. The third route leads you to a lookout point with a view that is open and stunning. There's a waist-high fence that helps you to feel safe and secure while you're observing the waterfall. Here, at last, you can truly relax, enjoy, and fully experience the magnificence of the waterfall in front of you.

Our children's lives are like the journey to the waterfall. There is so much beauty and excitement for them to take in and experience. But they have to learn to choose safe paths and stay within limits that let them fully experience all the wonder that life has to offer. So how do they discover these safe limits and boundaries and learn to make smart choices?

LIMITS TO BUILD INDEPENDENCE

One aspect of parenting that we put into effect early on is boundaries. We do many little things to protect our children when they're young: put them in cribs so that they won't roll onto the floor; install safety latches on cabinets to keep them away from poison; use car seats to keep them safe and secure while we drive. But, as they grow, we teach our kids boundaries by setting limits for them. This is important because we know their young minds are not mature enough to make the best choices, nor do they understand that choices often have consequences.

The first story of setting boundaries comes from the very first people in the Torah. Adam and Eve were told not to eat from one tree. Sure, they didn't understand exactly why God wanted them to avoid that specific tree. But they both experienced significant consequences by doing something they were specifically told not to do.

Setting boundaries provides our children with the safety and security they need while giving them some freedom to experience, grow, and enjoy life. As our kids continue to mature, we can change and broaden the boundaries we've put into place. This will allow them to develop "responsible independence," keeping some boundaries while ensuring that they're not suffocated or damaged by unreasonable restrictions. The key is to set limits that allow enough independence for them to develop and experience life fully.

Make no mistake; we're playing for big stakes here. Our children's future security, stability, and happiness depend on what we, as parents, do now. Of course, it's difficult to always know the right limits to set or to say no when it makes our children sad or angry. It often feels easier to not follow through because we want our children to be happy, to fit in, or to like us. Or maybe we're just plain tired of arguing. But while giving in is the easy way out (at least in the moment), our children will bear the long-term consequences if we let them go through life without experiencing healthy boundaries.

Let's explore this idea with a story about a boy who was very good at arguing with his parents when they tried to set limits. Eventually, his parents got tired of arguing and started regularly giving in to his demands. They even justified it by thinking that he could learn to be responsible by setting his own limits. As he got older, when they caught him sneaking out of the house in the middle of the night, his parents just talked to him about responsibility but imposed no consequences. Then, when they caught him smoking pot, they drew the line, telling him that it was not allowed in their house. However, they never addressed the issue of limits outside the home or future repercussions of this behavior, like health or legal issues.

This boy's parents finally woke up when he was arrested for selling pot in front of his school, but by then, it was too late to save him from the consequences of his actions. Unfortunately, many parents have seen their children experience damaging consequences of poor decisions they were allowed to make on their own.

If the parents had guided their son's behavior less with words and more through limits, rules, and boundaries, they could perhaps have changed the negative trajectory their son was on. Setting firm limits from the time our kids are young teaches them how to safely manage their own needs and behaviors, and the subsequent consequences of those behaviors.

Drawing boundaries around our children's decisions often means narrowing down their choices or steering them toward

Try This! SETTING LIMITS

An important first step to setting limits for our children is learning how to say "no" convincingly. How do we calmly, confidently, clearly, and lovingly say the word and mean it? When we examine this question in our workshops, parents are always surprised at how difficult it can actually be. We ask them to say the word "no" out loud, exactly the way they would say it to their kids. They usually discover how often they say the word with hesitation or with body language that actually says, "Well, maybe," even while the "no" is coming out. You don't need to be harsh, but you do want to be clear and sincere. Go ahead, look in the mirror, and see if your "no" comes out as clearly and confidently as your "yes" does. We know it's tough, but this is an important step. So start practicing saying a convincing "no!"

what we know are the wiser options. But sometimes it requires a hard "no," and it helps to remind ourselves that "no" is not a dirty word. Always giving in may make our children momentarily happy, but in the long run, catering to a child's every demand sends the wrong message. Helping children to realize that things won't always go their way is not only the responsible thing to do as parents, it's an extremely loving thing to do as well.

There are a few other factors to consider when setting limits for children. The limits (or boundaries) we put in place must be effective, reasonable, and healthy. It's always good to ask, "Is this limit needed?" or "What am I trying to accomplish with this?" You certainly don't want to become a parent who always says "no," because that handicaps children in a whole different way. Children still need to learn how to make their own wise choices. But when used carefully, appropriately, and with a good explanation, a gentle and firm "no" can bring security, strength, and courage to children as they grow.

LIMITS ARE LIKE FENCES

Setting limits has been a struggle as long as people have been around. We've already looked at the limits that gave Adam and Eve trouble, and we all can probably think of personal examples. The Bible tells us that "the soul is never satisfied" (Ecclesiastes 6:7). Everyone has areas of life in which putting limits is hard (it could be eating, shopping, drinking, sports, or anything else that's difficult for us personally). Limits are important all throughout life, which makes it even more important to teach them to our children when they're young, so they'll learn to limit themselves as they go through life.

The writers of *Pirkei Avot* thought this principle was so important for living a civilized and honorable life that they began their volume by warning teachers and leaders to "make a fence around the Torah" (*Pirkei Avot* 1:1). In Judaism, rules and regulations create this "fence," an extra level of stringency to safeguard and protect what's most important. For instance, because the Jewish Bible forbids buying and selling on Shabbat, early Jewish leaders forbade carrying money on Shabbat, lest a person accidentally come to perform this forbidden action.

Are most of the limits you've set up fair and reasonable? Would your kids agree?

This idea of protection applies as well to our families and in our homes. Putting up a fence provides a protective barrier between what is precious to us and what is unsafe or dangerous. Fences protect us, our family, and our valuables. Think about how much easier it is to prevent disaster than to undo the damage from a disaster after it has happened.

Knowing that we need fences—boundaries and limits—to protect our families and what we value doesn't mean we always know exactly where to place those fences. But we do know that it's human nature to go right up to the very edge of the fence and put ourselves dangerously close to the very thing we're trying to protect ourselves from. Think about what kids do at the zoo. They go right up and "test" the barrier, leaning over or even reaching their hands through the bars or chains of a fence. The zoo knows this, too, and therefore places the physical barrier far enough away from the potential danger so that direct contact with the animal is nearly impossible.

But because curiosity is a natural tendency in humans, it's also important not to build unreasonable fences. Do you think Adam and Eve would have paid much attention to that one specific tree if they hadn't been prohibited from eating its fruit? Not likely. Since it was forbidden, it came to seem more worthwhile than it actually was.

The same principle applies when we set limits for our children. If our limits are too rigid or controlling, our children may eventually want to rebel against them—and us. Having rules just for rules' sake is counterproductive; give kids too many *no*'s and they will start to tune you out. The brilliant medieval philosopher, doctor, and rabbi Maimonides put it wisely when he called the "path of the good," the trait of staying equidistant from two extremes (*Mishneh Torah*, Hilchot Deot 1:3).

SETTING THE RIGHT LIMITS

As mentioned above, setting limits is not just meant for the sake of having limits. The boundaries you set should matter to you and be implemented in a way that will make them effective. Establishing and maintaining effective boundaries takes time and effort, so make sure it's effort well spent.

Try to keep a positive attitude toward boundaries, and remain willing to modify them as life evolves and changes. Don't hesitate to revisit something that isn't accomplishing the goals you're trying to achieve.

Also know that there can be different levels of limits. Some limits are absolute walls prohibiting certain behavior (like using drugs), while others might start as walls and then evolve into more of a fence as children mature (like having a mobile phone). Crossing the street alone at age six is understandably forbidden, while at age sixteen, a parallel safety limit may involve a curfew. With age and maturity, kids' responsibilities can increase appropriately. At any age, the right combination of walls and fences can help prepare kids for both the challenges and risks of life.

Most teenagers today know about the danger of driving drunk or being a passenger in a car with a driver who has had too much to drink. But do they understand how much is too much? Teenagers are highly susceptible to peer pressure, so they shouldn't have to guess or spontaneously decide what choices to make in high-risk situations. It's much more effective to have specific rules laid out beforehand. Discuss this with them thoroughly and then create a fence, a wall, or a combination of the two that you think is most appropriate.

Drinking and driving is a clear example of how safety should not be compromised because of disapproval, hassle, or inconvenience. Kids may not understand (or like) the hard limits you set, but as they experience some benefits, they will begin to understand that limits really are in their own best interest. Sometimes, it can even be a relief for them to have an easy out and let you, their parents, become the bad guys.

To help determine where to set limits and what limits to set, it can be helpful to categorize specific areas of importance and concern for your family. The following is a list of areas we see as priorities, but these are only suggestions:

- Physical safety (like having a small child hold your hand when you cross the street or teaching your teenager never to get into a car with a friend who has been drinking)

- Emotional security (like not allowing name calling, teasing, or hitting; instead, speaking positive, affirmative words to each other)

- Respectful living (like asking permission before you borrow someone's clothes or having everyone pitch in to clean up after meals)

- Maintaining moral and religious values (like being present for Shabbat dinner or family gatherings, or every member of the family participating to help those in need)

CONNECTING LIMITS WITH RESILIENCE

How does setting limits build resilience in our children? Limits provide a smaller arena within which resilience can be nurtured and grow. Rather than have a whole field in which to learn, we fence in some of it; as kids grow and show their abilities, the fences get moved back. Pretty soon, children can handle the wider world with the built-in sense of limits and resilience that they have acquired this way.

Setting limits teaches children to grow into adults who can survive without the immediate gratification of having everything they want on demand. Limits also give parents a chance to provide guidance as children learn to handle challenges and disappointments.

Of course, we don't want or need to micromanage every aspect of our children's lives. It is often necessary to give kids the wiggle room they need to develop and learn. In a situation that is not physically or emotionally dangerous, sometimes it's better to see what choices children will make and how they will deal with what happens.

Give them opportunities to adapt in one of many small, every-day ways: allow them to do their own packing for a sleepover with a friend, manage their own money at an amusement park, set their own schedule to get to a movie on time, organize their own homework or extracurricular activities. It's entirely possible that they'll forget to pack a favorite piece of clothing or a toothbrush, miss the movie, or fail to leave enough time to do their homework so they have to miss some other activity.

Because we have allowed them to set their own limits in these small situations where there is no major danger, they'll learn from their mistakes, just like the rest of us. We can talk with them afterward about what they might do differently in the future. By letting them handle some of life's small (but enlightening) challenges and disappointments, they will learn how to handle themselves and will become better problem solvers.

That's the essence of resilience: being able to survive while learning how to get better results in similar future situations. We can give children some freedom and space to learn from small choices, while at the same time setting limits in order to protect them from larger choices that they are not yet able to developmentally or physically handle. Limits provide structure that will protect, comfort, and guide our children as they grow up.

We know it's difficult when they cry, have a temper tantrum, tell us they hate us, or compare us to their friends' parents. None of this is what we want to hear, and there will be times when it is easy to doubt or question what you are doing. But you can stand firm in the knowledge that you are acting in your children's long-term best interest. Giving them the strength of resilience will let them enjoy life, take on challenges, and handle the inevitable setbacks that come their way.

Let Children Experience Disappointments

One of the secrets to helping children develop resilience is allowing them to face hurdles and disappointments. By not rescuing our children from minor stumbling blocks, we help them develop coping skills. These coping skills will protect them from being overwhelmed when they encounter greater difficulty and adversity later in life.

This is a little like a vaccine. Most vaccines contain a tiny bit of whatever they're protecting us against. When our bodies are exposed to this small dose, we build immunity that protects us from the larger illness. In the same way, we let our kids experience the minor disappointments and challenges so they'll become stronger and better able to deal with bigger problems as they come along. This is the flipside of those small hurts and disappointments, what psychologist and author Wendy Mogel refers to as the "blessing of a skinned knee."

Of course we don't need to force our children into challenges that might be too much for them. But it's also advisable not to shield them from the problems that life brings at every age and stage, or rescue them from their own failures and responsibilities. Even though it might be tempting to call up a parent who didn't invite your child to a party, to blame a teacher for your child's low grade, or to become angry at a coach for not putting your kid in a game, resist this type of overprotective behavior.

FACING CHALLENGES BUILDS STRENGTH

Don't we all want to intervene, protect our children, and set them up for success? And if so, what's the harm in helping them out by persuading a coach or convincing a teacher on our child's behalf? It doesn't feel good when our kids are not recognized the way we think they should be. Whether they weren't chosen for the right sports team, didn't get the part in the school play, or didn't receive the grade we think they deserved, it seems reasonable to protest. After all, as parents, it's natural to want to protect them and fix their problems.

But jumping in doesn't do our children any favors. When we let them experience the (relatively) small disappointments of childhood without intervening, they become stronger and more capable of maintaining a good attitude. Not intervening doesn't mean that we don't care, or that we never step up if a situation is out of control. If a child does his or her best but a negative situation continues to escalate, we must use our judgment about when to intervene.

The main idea is that we care *more* about teaching them to stand up and speak out for themselves than we do about rescuing them from one particular situation. This helps children learn how to navigate relationships, while negotiating and dealing with disappointments. Of course, we will still be there to provide guidance on speaking up, getting feedback, and processing their disappointment...and be quick to intervene when our children have been treated in an inappropriate, unjust, or harmful way.

Keep in mind that children naturally react disproportionately to obstacles. So when your kids are pitching a fit about having to be home for your family dinner, eat matzah on Passover, or miss something fun with their friends on Yom Kippur, you may hear about how unfair you're being, and they'll beg you to give up your principles. Standing firm not only offers spiritual benefits; understanding these tenets of self-control and gaining the coping abilities that these habits will build into your children's personality will impact their entire future.

Helping Children Cope

While it is important to give children room to grow and to build their mechanisms for coping with disappointment, we can still listen and even help guide them through this process. To help them feel heard and understood, we can listen as they talk through their feelings about what's going on. Then, we can lovingly help them think through their options and guide them toward making the right choices. How can we accomplish this?

Listening

In chapter one, we addressed the importance of listening and communication in creating shalom bayit, a peaceful home. This is a slightly different idea—that simply by sharing a burden, it becomes lighter. How many times have you come home from a terrible day at work or simply out in the world and needed to "vent" to a spouse, partner, or friend? Once you had, even though nothing had changed about your day, you probably felt much better, simply because you'd been heard.

Think of a time your child experienced a major disappointment. How did you respond?

When we listen actively, we also help kids understand that while we're aware of what they are saying, we understand their situation, and we accept their perspective, we may not always rush in to intervene and interfere with their own developing tools of resilience. Here are some ideas to help you do just that:

- *Try not to overreact.* Pay attention to what your child is saying without getting emotional or upset. You don't need to judge or evaluate his thoughts for him.

- *Be objective and keep your feelings separate from your child's.* Give her time to express her feelings and get her story out without interrupting. You want your children to keep talking, especially as they move toward the teenage years.

- *Let your child have ownership of her own feelings.* Don't put yourself in her situation and comment on how you might feel; stay above it emotionally.

- *Don't push.* This isn't a time to ask a ton of questions or get every detail. Let your child talk only as much as he or she wants to.

- *Recognize that a child's feelings are often short-lived.* Dramatic emotions often lose their intensity once a child is able to vent them.

- *Don't have the "answer."* The point of active listening is to allow children to be heard in a nonjudgmental way so that they can eventually come to their own resolution.

Guiding

Once we've given kids a platform to share their thoughts and feelings by listening actively, we can help them think through what they can do about a situation, then guide them toward the best behavior and choices, both in the short and long term. When children are given strategies to solve their own problems, it helps them to cope with the challenges and disappointments life will inevitably bring their way.

Eleven-year-old Ali had a soccer game scheduled for the same day and time as a friend's birthday party. To her, this felt like an overwhelming choice—she was going to let someone down and risk a negative reaction from her friends. Obviously, Ali couldn't be in two places at once, and driving her back and forth was not an option.

As badly as Ali's mom wanted to interject her opinion, she asked guiding questions, letting her daughter think it through and choose which event to attend: "How do you think you'll feel afterward if you choose to go to the party?" "How do you think you'll feel afterward if you choose the soccer game?" "What's the downside/upside of going to the party?" "What's the downside/upside of going to the game?"

Using her mother as a sounding board, Ali was able to reach a conclusion on her own.

Every parent knows that childhood is full of little issues and dramas—though they may seem big to our kids. Blowing small obstacles out of proportion is actually a meaningful stage of the developmental process (think about how a two-year-old reacts to just about everything). So as we guide our children, it is important to demonstrate restraint and keep our own emotions in check, whether we are dealing with toddlers or teens, or any age in between. When your kids start complaining about a friend, teacher, coach, homework assignment, whatever, keep their age and developmental stage in mind and steer them toward dealing with the issue at hand. Work hard not to immediately dish out advice or minimize the problem.

If children share a problem or challenge they're facing, you may be tempted to change the subject, offer quick answers, or take control. These strategies may seem like the easiest and fastest ways to deal with the issue at hand (especially when in a hurry or when the problem seems trivial to you).

Of course, sometimes safety, health, or timing priorities mean that we must resolve a situation quickly. There are times when it's okay to have your two-year-old walk, and other times when you need to put him in a stroller and get going. But, when time isn't a factor, it's best to try to guide children toward resolving problems on their own.

Try responding with something like, "I wonder how you could...?" "What might be some options for dealing with this?" or "Is there anything else you can do?" This opens up dialogue rather than shutting it down with a quick answer. These responses encourage children to think and develop tools for dealing with obstacles. Then, we can help them evaluate their options before selecting the solution they think will work best.

If we can balance steering them in the right direction with giving them an appropriate amount of freedom to work out their own issues, our kids will develop more effectively and be more equipped to figure things out for themselves.

By encouraging and enabling your children to face challenges head-on, you are actually giving them a gift. Children who have learned how to cope with disappointment, and who can approach life's problems with confidence, have the courage to bounce back after defeat and overcome obstacles. And they have the confidence to grow into people who feel good about themselves and their capacity to meet challenges head-on.

Be Positive

The great Rabbi Shammai used to say, "Receive each person with a cheerful face" (*Pirkei Avot* 1:15). This advice has stood the test of time for over two thousand years.

Notice what Shammai didn't say: "Feel happy all the time," or "Always be cheerful." He also didn't say, "Don't worry, be happy." He was more realistic and instead steered us toward trying our best to look on the bright side of each situation. Expect the positive, Shammai's words imply, and we are more likely to receive it. Approaching negative people or situations with optimism can help make the best out of a less-than-ideal situation. Attitude matters, and choosing to approach difficult people or situations with an upbeat outlook can make a difference to the outcome, or at least to how we feel about it.

The way we interact with our children sets the tone for our whole relationship with them. Plus, it teaches them how to interact with others. Instilling positivity in our children can begin as simply as greeting them each morning and afternoon with a cheerful face, regardless of what kind of day we might be having or what our kids might have done wrong, like gotten into a fight at school or broken something valuable at home. If we believe that both we and they can overcome whatever has happened in the past, they will start believing the same thing.

When we aren't allowed to grow and get over past wrongs, we know we can wind up frustrated, disappointed, resentful, or even angry. Plus, our children are looking to us for security. If we put on a brave or optimistic face during difficult personal or family times, this can be a great source of strength and confidence for our children.

OFFERING ENCOURAGEMENT IN TOUGH TIMES

We all feel like giving up sometimes. Maybe we just don't know what to do next, are afraid of failing, feel completely overwhelmed, or can't see past a huge obstacle. Feelings like this are inevitable, but what matters most is what we do with these feelings. Do we carry on with the task at hand, or do we give up? Would it make a difference if someone was there to encourage us and tell us he or she believed we could do it? Sometimes, encouragement is all we need to give us the strength to take the next step (no matter how uncertain or scary it might be).

Children are no different. Putting on a cheerful face and projecting positive energy can help kids overcome difficult tasks or situations, just as it helps adults. Positivity and encouragement can build perseverance and resilience that will enable them not only to overcome the issue at hand but also build the skill of taking healthy risks, like trying out for a new sports team or going door-to-door to collect for a charitable organization (with different degrees of supervision, depending on age and ability).

BELIEVE CHANGE IS POSSIBLE

How can we can stay positive, even when things are tough? By believing that change is possible...because it really is. Every day is a new day, with new opportunities. If we aren't happy with our current circumstances, it is up to us to change them, find new opportunities, or find a way to rise above them. The first step is our attitude.

Think about all the famous examples we have of people overcoming obstacles with the right attitude. Michael Jordan didn't make his high school basketball team because he wasn't tall enough, J. K. Rowling's *Harry Potter and the Philosopher's Stone* was rejected by twelve publishing companies before being picked up, and Albert Einstein told his biographer, "My parents were worried because I started to talk comparatively late." It turned out they didn't need to worry about young Albert's intellectual abilities, Michael Jordan grew tall enough after all, and Rowling's rejected manuscript became the fastest-selling book series of all time.

There are also great examples of overcoming obstacles in the Torah. Moses had a speech impediment, yet he still was able to lead the children of Israel out of slavery in Egypt. When Joshua and Caleb returned from their spying mission and were the only two who believed the Israelites would be able to conquer the land of Canaan, they faced enormous pressure to change their minds and comply with the other spies who believed it would be too difficult.

We've all heard the phrase "mind over matter," perhaps so often that we believe it's a cliché that can't apply to our specific situation. But the truth is that the thoughts in our head are what fill our heart. And this is what ultimately fuels and motivates us. Believing change is possible helps us persevere through challenging situations or overcome obstacles standing in the way of accomplishment.

This is also true of our own parenting abilities. Everyone benefits if we believe that we can improve, and move our thoughts and actions in a healthy, positive direction. By modeling this, our children will learn to believe they can take actions to make things better in their lives.

Jewish teaching promotes optimism about people and their potential to change for the better through the concept of *teshuvah*, "repentance." The Talmud states that if we do teshuvah out of love, we can transform our mistakes into *mitzvot*, positive and even Godly actions (Talmud, *Yoma* 86b). The word *teshuvah* actually means "return," which tells us that it's never too late to change. So not only is it important for us as adults to believe change is possible; it is important for our children to realize that we believe in them as well.

Often, simple changes in the way we speak to our children can make an enormous difference. If your children forget a chore, reminding them in a positive way will help to minimize conflict. Instead of saying, "If you don't remember to take out the trash next time, you'll be punished," try phrasing this in a positive way: "I know you'll remember to take out the trash next time."

Another scenario might find you sounding just like your own parents as you rant, "I am sick and tired of your messy room! If you don't clean it this weekend, you're in big trouble." Try wording it more like, "We have a busy weekend with a lot to do around the house, and I know I can count on you to help by taking care of your room."

The first statements in the scenarios above are scolding and imply that we don't believe our kids are really capable of changing. The second statements are positive ones that let them know that we not only believe that they can change, but that we expect it of them.

We're not suggesting that you shouldn't set consequences for your children's actions. The scenarios are meant to demonstrate how shifting the tone from negative to positive expectations can make a difference and cut down on conflict.

PLAN FOR THE FUTURE

Jewish tradition looks toward the future in a positive way. When the Israelites grumbled in the desert and wanted to return to Egypt, Moses spoke to them enthusiastically about the land of Canaan, filled with milk and honey. He understood that cultivating optimism in a visually compelling way was as important as food and water for his people. And he knew that making the future tangible, by being clear, articulate, and descriptive about the good things that would happen, was the best way to embrace optimism.

As parents, we want our children not only to believe in themselves, but also to know that we believe they'll achieve their goals. Helping them create positive, encouraging, and upbeat visions can inspire and motivate them. And positivity is an important antidote to the corrosive effects that pessimism can have on our kids' resilience.

Often, building positivity comes one step at a time. We can teach children that even though they might only advance one small step at a time, slow and steady progress will eventually lead to their desired goal or outcome. Long-term objectives are achieved by taking all of the necessary short-term steps. We want children to understand that managing the factors that are under their control now (the smaller, daily tasks) will help them to take the small steps needed to build toward longer-term goals. So let's look at some scenarios:

1. *Goal:* to improve a child's grades by the end of the year.

   First step: with your child, look at the subject that he or she is struggling with. Then, talk through any issues (lack of understanding, time constraints, etc.) that might be affecting his or her grades. Help identify an action he or she will take to overcome a specific obstacle and create a specific plan (such as talking with teachers, doing extra homework, or taking a different approach to studying) that your child will follow moving forward.

   Follow-up: check in with your child (daily at first, then weekly, then as needed) about how he or she is following the plan and how schoolwork and grades are progressing.

2. *Goal:* to get along better with siblings.

   First step: sit children down when a conflict arises and talk through what started the conflict, how each child is feeling, and how they think their sibling is feeling. Then have a conversation with them about steps they can each take to avoid the same conflict in the future. Also make it clear what kinds of reactions and responses to provocation are and are not acceptable to you. Many families we know have a "no physical response" rule.

   Follow-up: when conflict starts to build, remind them of the steps they can take to tone things down. Make sure to praise efforts they take toward avoiding, minimizing, or resolving conflict on their own. See chapter four for more about the problem-solving process.

3. *Goal:* to make a certain sports team.

    First step: talk through the specific skills and attitudes your child needs to excel at the desired sport. Then have your child think of what he or she might do to help the team, as well what he or she can do to stand out and improve his or her own skills. Set a timeline or plan that your child can work through to improve and build his or her skill level.

    Follow-up: help create the time and space for carrying out the plan. Keep checking in on your child's practice, progress, and success in improving his or her skill level (and when time allows, work with your child).

We help our kids develop resilience by responding to setbacks or challenges in their lives with encouragement and realistic action plans. That's our job—we want our kids to know we believe in them, but we also don't want them to overreach. We prepare them to realize that their actions won't guarantee a specific grade or control what decisions coaches make. But we have confidence in their abilities, and we are proud of them for taking steps toward their goals.

Teaching children to set goals for what they want to get done on a daily, weekly, or monthly basis reinforces that you believe they can accomplish things. You can support them in the process by creating "to do" lists, talking through how best to accomplish what is on the list, and making necessary changes to keep the list realistic.

Yes, "to do" lists actually can help to build resilience! How? By showing kids that they have the capacity to accomplish things, even things that might be difficult and take some time—and many small steps—to work out.

Of course, it's important to be flexible and realistic about goals. Good communication between parent and child is critical, so work actively to keep interaction positive while sharing your thoughts and goals, and listen to your children's thoughts and feelings. Remember, there is a big difference to kids between "checking in" and "checking up on." Strive for the former, as that breeds self-confidence.

And as anyone with middle-school-aged children knows, it's vitally important that we practice what we preach. This is the age when they are keenly attuned to any whiff of hypocrisy in their parents. "Do as I say, not as I do" absolutely won't work with middle-schoolers. As with every area covered by this book, it's important for us to start modeling early the behavior we want to see in our children.

We can intentionally demonstrate and practice the behaviors, attitudes, and actions we want our kids to exhibit. Share your own challenges (with work, with friends, with family, with your synagogue or other organizations) to show children how you are setting goals and making plans to try to improve various situations. You can even offer to have your kids check in on your progress, or, at the very least, discuss your progress with them and any changes you need to make in your approach. Coauthor Maurice J. Elias once served as chairperson of his synagogue's religious school board, and he asked his children, who were then attending the school, to help him create a plan for dealing with students coming late and leaving early. His children had good ideas and were in a position to be his on-site reporters regarding how the plans were working out.

Try This! TAKE AN OPTIMISM BREAK

Give yourself (and your kids) an Optimism Break! When frustration is boiling over and your child risks becoming discouraged from a stressful, intensive task, taking a two- to ten-minute break can help him or her gain a sense of perspective. Much as we may feel that pushing through is the best solution, sometimes letting children take a few minutes to forget the stress and frustration can help them feel good about themselves. They can play an instrument, draw a picture, build with Legos, or shoot a few baskets. This can give them the boost they need to attack the task again with renewed energy, sparking creativity and gaining a fresh perspective. Be firm about the allotted break time to prevent abuse. But be sure to offer another break before long.

Discussing obstacles, setting a plan, and having the family as a support system will make the necessary efforts seem more manageable and will also protect our kids from becoming demoralized at any setback. Disappointments will still come, but it's a lot easier to bounce back when the letdown is relatively small and doesn't feel like a total failure. Through this process, you're also giving children small accomplishments to feel proud of every day. This is more powerful and effective than hinging all of their hopes on one big success, because it's not always possible to guarantee complete success.

Know How to Laugh

Imagine you're almost one hundred years old, and suddenly you're told that you're going to have a baby. Hilarious, right? That's exactly what happened in the Bible to Sarah, Abraham's wife. She was close to one hundred when she was told that she was about to bear a son. And what did she do (probably after fainting)? She laughed. The Bible gives so much emphasis to this laughter that Abraham and Sarah ended up giving their son a name that means "laughter" in Hebrew—Yitzchak (Isaac).

Unfortunately, in our frenzied culture, we miss out on many of the rewards of laughter. Too many households feel so much pressure that they don't see the value and importance in humor. They see it as silly, foolish, or unproductive, which leaves them functioning within a hurried, monotone, serious atmosphere. And missing out on humor in life creates children who are impatient, overscheduled, and grumpy.

Not too many things are repeated in Jewish texts, but when they are, we know they are important. In *Pirkei Avot*, a few pages after the verse "Receive each person with a cheerful face" (1:15) we are told, "Receive every person with happiness" (3:16). A later tradition teaches, "If you give your fellow all the best gifts in the world with a grumpy face, Scripture regards it as if you had given the person nothing. But when you receive your fellow with a cheerful face, even if you give nothing at all, Scripture credits you as though you had given the person all the best gifts in the world" (*Avot De-Rabbi Natan* 13:4).

Even in difficult circumstances, humor and laughter can be valuable tools. We've all heard the saying "Laughter is the best medicine." Having a sense of humor, no matter what life dishes out, is definitely good for your health.

Science is only now catching up with Jewish tradition. Researchers are studying the specific effects of humor and playfulness on our bodies. When we laugh, our heart rates go up, immune systems are activated, hormones are pumped, our alertness increases, blood flow improves, and oxygen goes to the brain, which can make our thought processes sharper and increase our ability to see things with greater clarity. Humor relaxes our skeletal muscles and helps our digestive systems work better, both of which lead to even more physical and psychological benefits. Stress levels go down, tension and hostility lessen, and we are more capable of feeling empathy and broadening our perspective. So, naturally, our ability to make sound decisions and resolve conflicts improves.

Laughter also is an incredible bonding agent and remedy to family stress, something well known to Jewish families through years of harsh oppression. There are many stories of how laughter and song provided lifelines to families during times of slavery, famine, and migration. Families who laugh together usually enjoy being around one another more. Humor gives us the freedom to express imperfect ideas and make mistakes without the fear of being ridiculed. We can lighten up our lives by lightening up our households.

Harnessing the power of laughter is a basic tenet of smart Jewish parenting. We've long observed that laughter can be found in the middle of tragedy. Look at how we celebrate Purim. It's a holiday filled with joy and merriment, but what's so joyous about commemorating a plot to destroy the entire Jewish people? The root of the humor lies in the irony that the very person (Haman) determined to destroy the Jewish nation was instead crushed by the very thing he created to abolish it. And thus, the holiday of Purim became one of laughter.

Here are some tips for utilizing humor anywhere. The first letter of each of the first five tips spell out the word *laugh*, to help you remember, or perhaps just to make you smile a little. These five tips are shared with permission from Dr. Ed Dunkelblau of the Institute for Emotionally Intelligent Learning.

- **L**augh heartily whenever possible with your children, spouse, and friends.

- **A**pproach the world around you with amazement. Try to see everything in new ways and from different perspectives. Judaism reinforces this with traditional blessings when we see a rainbow or the first time we eat a fruit in season.

- **U**se aids to help increase your daily total of laughs. Be creative and silly. Have comedy CDs or podcasts in the car or store some funny tracks on your smartphones and tablets; create a funny family video or watch a funny TV show each week together; doing this together is a great bonding experience. Some families have a specific place in their house for silly behavior or read funny books (for younger kids, Dr. Seuss books are great, as well as the Jewish folk tales based on the silly wise men of Chelm).

- **G**ive yourself time for fun. Game playing is worth the time. Taking time to learn to play games—especially games that are not on the computer, such as card games, dreidel, or Scrabble or other board games—leads to fun and family building.

- "**H**umor buddies" are to be cherished. These are the people in your life who are funny, playful, and perhaps a bit irreverent. Be sure to get a regular dose of these people, and be sure your children are exposed to them as well. Help your children find and keep friends who like to laugh and who make your children laugh.

Here are some more ideas we have found helpful in building resilience through humor:

- *Let yourself go*—lighten up and let loose on the holidays that are specifically designed for us to have fun. The Jewish holidays of Simchat Torah and Purim are two great examples. On Simchat Torah, we are expected to rejoice—to sing and dance with the Torah and let ourselves find great joy in what we have been given. On Purim, beyond laughter, we are expected to be outright silly, to dress up in costumes, and to play games. Don't just dress your kids up; let them see you dress up. The sages who passed down these traditions knew how important humor, laughter, and fun were to life. They knew that life isn't about waiting to have fun until we are "happy" but to make the best out of, and find joy in, every situation.

- *Search your environment for things to laugh at daily.* Your smiles and cheerful expressions are also contagious; so try to infect others with humor!

- *Take a Laughter Test.* Do you and your family still have the ability to giggle? How about a full-on belly laugh? In the book *Emotionally Intelligent Parenting: How to Raise a Self-Disciplined, Responsible, Socially Skilled Child,* authors Maurice J. Elias, Steven E. Tobias, and Brian S. Friedlander ask families to test themselves by reading the following paragraph aloud. It can be done by each family member, one at a time, or by everyone together:

  Ha ha ha ha ha ha. Hee hee hee. Har-de-har-har. Nyuck nyuck nyuck. Ho ho ho ho. Ha ha hee hee har har nyuck ho ho. Tee hee hee hee ha ha ho ho ho ho ho ha ha ha ha ha. Nyuck nyuck nyuck. Ha ha ha ha har-de-har ho ho ho hee hee hee hee giggle giggle ha ha. Ho ho ho ho ho ha ha ha ha hee hee hee. Ha ha. Ha!

WHY ARE WE DOING THIS?

Before the Talmudic sage Rabbah would begin a lecture, he would crack a joke to make all the other rabbis laugh. Rabbah would then sit down to begin his lecture (Talmud, *Pesachim* 117a). By doing this, he set a tone of joy and humor to lighten up the mood and make the studies more enjoyable. And we can

Try This! BUILDING POSITIVITY

Make a box of hugs. Take something small, like an empty baby wipes box, and decorate it with your child. Then, together, make a set of Hug Cards, on blank index cards, which entitle the person who picks a card to get a specific kind of hug. You can even have your child decorate or draw a picture on the card. Human touch is important. And hugs heal. Hugs help keep a family together. Hugs are a safe way of sharing warm feelings. Some examples of hug cards:

- A Hug and a Cookie (first comes the hug, then, you share a favorite cookie)

- A Mommy Hug or a Daddy Hug

- A Grandparent Hug (these can be saved and redeemed when a visit takes place)

- A Kid Hug (which could involve one sibling hugging another)

- A Club Sandwich Hug (where the person who picks the card is in the middle, and everybody else gathers around to give the hug)

- A Hug and a Hum (while giving a hug, the person hums a song)

(Continues on next page)

- A Hug and a Prayer (or blessing, or other positive saying or wish)

- A Hug and a Hop (hop together while hugging)

- A High-Five Hug or a Low-Five Hug

- A No-Touch-But-Get-as-Close-as-You-Can Hug

- A BIG Hug or a little hug

- A Loud Hug or a Hug and a Buzz (make a buzzing sound during the hug)

- A Hug and a Mug (after the hug, share a cup of hot chocolate, hot apple cider, or warm milk)

- A Hug of Your Choice

Use these ideas or create your own, incorporating what works for your family. Change it up every once in a while to keep the ideas fresh. You can even get your teens involved, as long as you don't require them to admit that they like it (which most do) or ever tell their friends that they participated.

do this in our own homes, using humor to build a happier, more bonded household.

Judaism teaches that all people are made in God's image and also that "the One who sits in heaven laughs" (Psalm 2:4). Thus, the ability to laugh is something sacred, part of the essence of who we are and our connection to our Creator. It's a central part of our capacity to live. Laughter has helped the Jewish people endure grief and sorrow while always moving forward. Laughter can strengthen our relationships and fill us up emotionally. It gives us and our children joy, energy, tenacity, and resilience. The more we laugh, the better we live.

Even after almost one hundred years of childlessness, Sarah never lost her capacity to laugh. We can draw inspiration from her and laugh as much as we can through this amazing roller coaster called parenting. It's a key building block toward creating resilience, both for ourselves and for our children.

Wrap-Up

We close this chapter by reminding ourselves that resilience protects our children throughout their lives. It helps preserve their minds and spirits from being crushed by the inevitable disappointments, failures, and pains we cannot possibly shield them from. Sherri Mandell, author of *The Road to Resilience: From Chaos to Celebration*, sums it up beautifully when she writes, "Resilience is really the story of the Jewish people. Through our long and tortuous history, we continue to bounce back, to move forward. But resilience doesn't just mean bouncing back; it means growing greater."

This is the essence of why resilience is so important. It isn't simply surviving; it's the process of growing greater, stronger, more formidable. And dare we say, the greater our capacity to be resilient and embrace the fullness of life, the greater our probability of experiencing joy.

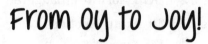

From Oy to Joy!

You'll know that you are moving from oy to joy when your child…

- forgets her lines in the play but bounces back faster than you expected—even more determined to succeed next time.

- pushes the limits you have set but backs off more easily than you expected when you hold your ground and explain your reasoning.

- does a ridiculous-looking dance move to try to make you and his siblings laugh.

- cooperates to set realistic, measurable goals, like tidying her room once a week.

chapter 4

Promote Responsibility

"If I am not for myself, who will be for me?

And if I am only for myself, then what am I?

And, if not now, when?"

—*Pirkei Avot 1:14*

"You cannot escape the responsibility of

tomorrow by evading it today."

—*Abraham Lincoln*

■ ■ ■

A group of campers was preparing for their first campout. Noticing that they seemed to be having a lot of trouble getting organized to go out into the woods, their counselor asked, "Have you forgotten any essential equipment?" One boy replied, "Yes, my mother."

■ ■ ■

We can laugh at this because we know how true it is. Yet by teaching our kids how to be independent and to assume responsibility for themselves we give them a system for successfully traveling through life. Teaching a child to swim appears on the Talmud's list of things a parent is obligated to do (Talmud, *Kiddushin* 29a). The broader lesson is that teaching kids to be responsible for their own survival is a critical part of our own task.

How do we instill the trait of responsibility in our kids? And what exactly does the term "responsible" mean? How much and what type of responsibility do we want our kids to have?

Responsibility means being able to make decisions about our actions without anyone else's approval—and being responsible for the consequences of those actions. However, being responsible can also include the following:

- Being dependable (reliable and trustworthy)

- Keeping your word and meeting your commitments

- Being accountable for behavior (recognizing and acknowledging mistakes)

- Making contributions to your family, community, and the world

- Performing to the best of your ability

Most parents, when asked, will list responsibility as one of the qualities they most want their children to possess. We already know how important the many skills that make up our children's sense of responsibility will be for success in school, relationships, work, and in life. As it says in the Book of Proverbs, "Train a child in the way he should go, and even when he is old, he will not depart from it" (Proverbs 22:6).

But teaching children to accept and demonstrate responsibility can be challenging. When babies are born, they're incapable of doing anything for themselves, and it is our job not only to meet their physical needs, but also to protect them, keeping them safe and content. So we nurture, coddle, and cocoon them in a safe little world. But as children grow, they learn that they are not the center of the universe and that the world does not revolve around them (God forbid!). Soon enough, they will face the opportunities, challenges, temptations, and risks that demand that they learn to take care of themselves.

Our first instinct might be to shield them from the ups and downs of life, but this is not realistic, nor is it helpful to our children. Ultimately, we want them to become responsible for themselves as well as responsible members of their communities. That's why we must build their skills and behaviors of reliability and dependability. This is the same message the Israelites sent to the prophet Ezra when they wanted him to assume leadership: "Arise, for it is your task, and we are with you; be strong and do it" (Ezra 10:4).

So how can we help our children "be strong and do it"? How do we teach kids responsibility so they'll grow into fully functioning adults, with successful relationships and careers? Let's explore a few strategies to help them develop the indispensable attribute of responsibility:

- Nurture responsibility at home

- Contribute locally and globally

- Promote accountability

- Practice problem solving

Nurture Responsibility at Home

The first step is to make sure we, as parents, provide an environment that nurtures responsibility. As with so many other things, this begins with what we model. Are *we* responsible, reliable, and trustworthy? Do we respect other people's time and property? Do we fulfill our commitments to the best of our ability? Most importantly, do we do what we tell our children we are going to do? Do we keep our promises? By modeling these behaviors, we're taking an important step toward raising responsible children. As *Pirkei Avot* reminds us, "The essential thing is not study but deed" (*Pirkei Avot* 1:17). It's less about what we say and more about what we do that makes all the difference in the world.

Watching you, would your child say you are a responsible person?

Beyond modeling it ourselves, how else can we raise a capable and confident child who is consistent, dependable, and trustworthy? It all starts with the home environment we create. As in the game of tag, home is where we always have to get back to, our safe haven, the base from which all of our journeys begin. And the way we create our home is an expression of the values that matter most to us, which we will nurture, encourage, and build in our children. Judaism places great value on the community and how we support and take responsibility for each other. Our homes are micro-communities where we can help our children to:

- *Feel needed:* We can let our children help us, even when they are very young. It might take a few extra minutes for them to sort out their stuffed animals and put them away in the proper bins, and their rooms might not come out perfectly, but look at how satisfied they'll feel when they take responsibility for the condition of the home they live in. Add chores as they grow, in line with your family's needs, like taking out the trash, picking up after themselves, or clearing the table after a meal.

- *Feel appreciated:* As we will discuss in the chapter on gratitude, everyone needs to feel appreciated. It's no different when kids help out. Since younger kids usually love to help, if we combine letting them pitch in with letting them know how helpful they are to us, they'll develop a sense of pride that could blossom into future initiative.

- *Feel capable:* As we noted in the chapter on resilience, children need to feel empowered to handle challenges and solve problems. They must believe they can accomplish things on their own. Think of how proud kids are when they finally get the knack of tying their shoes or riding a two-wheeler for the first time. Of course, this confidence and pride inspires them to keep repeating the behavior. Imagine if the same thing could happen while they were helping around the house!

- *Feel like a part of a team:* Most of the time, when we know others are depending on us, we step up and do what needs to be done. We're more likely to accept responsibility when we feel like our efforts mean something to other people. Families are like teams, and teams do their best when everyone has a valued role, even a small one.

- *Understand consequences:* Kids also need to learn that it's their responsibility to take care of their things and live up to family expectations, as part of the family "community." If they don't, there will be consequences. Remember the section on setting limits in the chapter on resilience? That also applies here. We need to follow through on the expectations we have laid out for our kids—even if it means that they will be sad or angry for a while. Consequences could mean that a child loses a toy because he or she refuses to put it away, or loses computer or TV privileges for visiting a site or watching a program that isn't allowed. Establishing consequences in advance shows children that their choices lead directly to these outcomes; they are not just capricious punishments imposed by "mean" parents.

Two skills that help us nurture responsibility in our children at home are understanding what is appropriate for their age and skill level and encouraging constant—even daily—practice.

TAKE ON APPROPRIATE RESPONSIBILITY

Parents usually know what their kids are capable of. Try to share new responsibilities with a light, cheerful tone: "Avi, starting today, you're going to make your bed in the morning before you go to school. I have a lot of other things to do in the morning, like getting everyone's lunch ready; it will be very helpful to me not to have to tidy up your bed."

Demonstrate patiently how tasks should be done—knowing that kids won't always get it exactly right at first. The goal is taking responsibility, not perfection. "After you are dressed, take your pillows off like this, and pull the sheet and cover all the way to this corner. Make sure the sheet and cover haven't come out over here—see how it has gotten loose? When that happens, just tuck it in like this, fluff the pillow like this, and put it on top. And that's it! It will take you a minute, and it will be a big help to me."

Once we've established an environment where responsibility can blossom, we need to determine what level of responsibility our child is capable of taking on. As children get older and their abilities in other areas grow and develop, their understanding and aptitude for responsible behavior should also grow. What does this look like in practice?

If we start when they are young, kids are more likely to have a good attitude about it (at least, most of the time). If you're just starting to implement this process with children who are a little older, then it might be best to progress gradually toward both helpfulness and a better attitude, expecting slight resistance along the way. Obviously, when children are babies, we don't expect them to help. But even a young child can start to do little things, like picking up her toys or putting his sippy cup into the sink. As they grow, kids can take on more responsibilities and larger tasks as they develop.

Looking at the scenario of clearing the table after dinner, a child's responsibilities might progress something like this as he or she ages:

- Put sippy cup in the sink

- Gather napkins from the table

- Collect plates and put them by the sink

- Rinse plates

- Rinse and load dishes in dishwasher

Increasing responsibility levels in children helps shape habits that will affect them for the rest of their lives. Children who are never expected to assume responsibility are more likely to grow up feeling entitled to anything they want. They may even begin to resent the slightest imposition on them. And kids who are just taught a minimal amount of responsibility might learn to do the least possible with a not-so-great attitude, which does not translate into productive adult behavior. Think about how your child's attitude today might translate to an assignment in college, a project at work, or future family responsibilities.

When our kids view helping out as contributing to a team (the family) and know that their efforts are important and appreciated, this encourages more and more responsible, helpful behavior. Then, we'll have lots of opportunities to kvell (burst with pride) about how we are raising such a mensch (a person of integrity and dependability). Oh the joy, for any parent, Jewish or otherwise, to sit back and watch their kids taking on and successfully handling new responsibilities!

PRACTICE EVERY DAY

Imagine your child going away to summer camp and getting stuck with a bunkmate who refused to do anything because he or she had a full-time maid at home. This kid's bed was never made, clothes were in everyone else's space, empty food wrappers were thrown around, and the entire cabin risked losing privileges because of this one child's mess. Would your child be angry and resent losing privileges or feel forced to pick up after this bunkmate?

As an adult, have you ever felt resentful of people who weren't "pulling their own weight"— at work, in the synagogue, or in any another organization? Most likely, you have.

Becoming a responsible person takes intention; changing behaviors and habits doesn't just happen overnight. Fortunately, the home and the community provide a wide range of opportunities to help our children develop this important quality.

With our hectic schedules, there are even more opportunities for our kids to practice responsible behavior. Many of our daily activities—eating, playing, wearing clean clothes—require multiple smaller tasks. If no one goes to the grocery store or cooks, what are we going to eat? If no one does laundry, what will we wear? Is it only the parent's responsibility to make sure these daily tasks get done?

Work, school, sports, and other activities contribute to our chaotic schedules. To deal with this, some families hire help to keep up homes and yards. Does that mean that no one else should make daily contributions to the home and family? There are—and always should be—daily tasks for which our children can begin to take responsibility. Think through specific tasks or chores that might be motivating and encouraging. Here are a few suggestions to help you define expectations within your family:

- Choose jobs that have an immediate positive impact.

- Choose not only tasks that help the child directly (such as tidying his or her room) but also those that help the family in general (such as organizing or taking out the recycling, or setting the table for Shabbat).

- Choose age-appropriate, realistic tasks.

- Show your appreciation for your child's contribution and acknowledge a job well done.

- After ensuring that everybody is on board and willing to assume responsibility for its care, get a family pet and delegate tasks for looking after it. (According to Jewish law, one must feed one's pet before feeding oneself.)

- Use special times (like Shabbat and holidays) as opportunities to give kids more responsibility, like helping to plan menus, doing some cooking, setting the table, taking out the challah cover and board, polishing the candlesticks, etc.

Nothing teaches responsibility better than real-life experiences, and home is the best place to start. Not only will our kids

Try This! PRACTICE RESPONSIBILITY

Organize a family workday, indoors or out, for all the things you've been putting off. This works well for spring- or Passover cleaning. Airing and preparing camping and boating supplies or ski and snowboard equipment also make great seasonal projects, as does yard work of any kind. Make sure every family member has responsibilities he or she can handle and knows how to complete effectively (it doesn't have to be perfect). Let kids know that everyone's work will be celebrated with a fun family outing once the job is done.

learn to take care of themselves, there's the added bonus of making life a bit easier on us as parents. But as a note of caution: try not to fall into the trap of getting kids started on a job and then stepping in to finish the task yourself when you see that they are not doing it properly or efficiently. Picture this scene:

Mom is baking and getting the house ready for guests. Seven-year-old Sarah volunteers to vacuum. Mom sees that Sarah isn't getting all the way under the chairs. She stops what she's doing and takes away the vacuum.

Mom: I'll just do it quickly myself.

Sarah: Mom, why can't I do it? I love to vacuum.

Mom: You won't be able to get all the stuff off the floor, especially under the chairs.

Sarah: I can, Mom. Let me try. I'll show you how good I am.

Mom: No, Sarah, you'll take too long. I can do it a lot faster myself.

What message did Sarah get from this interaction? Probably that she wasn't capable or fast enough. Do you think this will make her eager to help next time? Here's another version of the same scenario:

Mom is baking and getting the house ready for guests. Seven-year-old Sarah volunteers to vacuum. Mom sees that Sarah isn't getting all the way under the chairs. Mom stops what she's doing.

Mom: I'll just vacuum quickly myself.

Sarah: Mom, why can't I do it? I love to vacuum.

Mom: You know what? You really do love to help out.

Sarah: I can, Mom. Let me try. I'll show you how good I am.

Mom: Okay, you're right. We're not in that much of a hurry.

Sarah: Look, I never noticed all these crumbs under the chairs. I'd better vacuum under there, too.

Mom: You're doing great. Thanks for your help, Sarah. I really appreciate it.

Luckily, in this second scenario, Sarah's mom rethought her position and listened. Sure, she could have vacuumed faster and probably made the floor more spotless than Sarah. But what was more important here? That the floors be perfect or that Sarah learns responsibility? And how can Sarah learn without the opportunity to practice and improve?

Let's now look at ways we can teach our children to contribute on a larger scale by venturing out of the house and into the world around them.

Contribute Locally and Globally

Judaism is all about community. Through life celebrations, mourning rituals, and holidays, the community comes together in mutual support. The bar or bat mitzvah demonstrates this, coming at exactly the age when a child is ready to start appreciating the rights and responsibilities he or she is given in the Jewish community. Responsibility in Judaism is not only a personal and family commitment, but also a community social and moral obligation. *Pirkei Avot* reminds us that "it is not your responsibility to finish the work, but you are not free to desist from it either" (*Pirkei Avot* 2:21).

Contributing to both local communities and the larger world is a central part of Judaism, and we can teach our children how to effectively participate. The Talmud says, "All Jews are responsible for one another" (Talmud, *Shevu'ot* 39a). The ideas of being our "brother's keeper" (Genesis 4:9) and "loving your neighbor as yourself" (Leviticus 19:18) have also guided us for millennia. These principles are cornerstones of community life.

Every day, we have opportunities to model behavior and teach our children specific ways to contribute to our local and global communities. Two concrete Jewish concepts can guide us as we try to impart this value to our children—*tikun olam* and *bal tashchit*.

REPAIRING THE WORLD: TIKUN OLAM

Tikun olam literally means "repairing the world," making it a better place. This belief embraces social action, looking out for the welfare of other people, not just as a "nice idea" that is optional, but as an obligation to our fellow human beings. Tikun olam demands that we be willing to look beyond ourselves—and actually do it. In the words of Anne Frank, "How wonderful it is that no one need wait a single moment before starting to improve the world."

It may be a cliché, but it remains true that the path to thinking globally is to start locally. This larger expression of responsibility starts with small, everyday steps we can take very close to home.

Here are a few ways of performing tikun olam in your community today:

- Providing food for or entertaining people in assisted living

- Gathering used toys or clothes to donate to kids in need

- Volunteering at a homeless shelter or soup kitchen, or running a food drive

- Visiting seniors who are housebound

- Packing backpacks of school supplies for children in developing countries

- Buying new clothes or collecting used ones for needy kids in your area

- Speaking out or demonstrating against an injustice in your community

- Preparing snack bags to be distributed among homeless people

- Making holiday or get-well cards for a local children's hospital

- Joining in other community service projects, such as a community clean-up day

The joy of knowing we are making a difference, coupled with actually seeing a positive impact on others, can inspire in ourselves and our children an increased desire to do more and to make a larger impact. What an amazing thing to teach children—that small, individual efforts can change another person's life and help make our entire community better. In the often-quoted words of anthropologist Margaret Mead, "Never doubt that a small group of thoughtful, committed citizens can change the world. Indeed, it's the only thing that ever has."

NOT DESTROYING: BAL TASHCHIT

Another Jewish concept of responsibility is *bal tashchit*, which literally means "do not destroy." It comes from the Torah passage forbidding people to cut down or destroy the fruit trees of an enemy town (Deuteronomy 20:19). Here, the Torah is teaching us that even if it's to our advantage (in this case, to gain military control), we can't destroy a natural part of the world that is essential for human survival.

The modern practice of bal tashchit focuses on environmental responsibility and on being mindful of long-term impacts of wasteful behavior and overconsumption. In this specific way, we can deliberately and thoughtfully work toward a healthier, more stable planet.

Because we benefit from this planet's resources, it is also our responsibility to preserve and protect it from damage and decay. Earth's gifts didn't come with a guarantee that they would last forever. The way we treat our natural resources has direct consequences for their sustainability. The impact of air and water pollution, deforestation, greenhouse gases, global warming, and extinction all have been well documented.

So it has become a central Jewish value to treat our environment with respect, to help repair damage, and to take care not to cause more. And again, this repair begins locally, at home with our children. Steps we can take to fulfill the value of bal tashchit in our families include:

- Recycling at home

- Repurposing used containers such as glass bottles

- Tracking and conserving natural resources (like water)

- Monitoring (with kids' help!) our family's use of electricity, fuel, and water

- Appreciating food by not wasting it (taking only what we will eat)

- Understanding the mentality of overconsumption in our society

- Becoming politically active on environmental issues

- Supporting environmental causes by volunteering or with donations

In the words of Teddy Roosevelt, "Do what you can, with what you have, where you are." In March, many synagogues have "mitzvah days," when children, parents, and others come together to do projects to help those in need. Whether it's making food baskets or soup for the hungry, bringing toys and books to children in hospitals, making decorated thank-you notes for first responders, or working on a community garden, the key is that these projects are homemade (the toys and books are gently used from children's homes), not purchased. The doing is accompanied by explaining the meaning of the action, at the appropriate level for our kids.

The Jewish concepts of tikun olam and bal tashchit instill a belief in social responsibility, of doing the right thing for the right reasons without thought of reward. This will help our children understand the inseparable bond between their own well-being and the well-being of others.

Promote Accountability

One giant step toward becoming more responsible is helping our kids recognize how their actions affect other people and gradually holding them accountable for both the good and the bad consequences of their actions.

Have you ever known adults who refuse to take responsibility for their actions? Nothing is ever their fault, they can never be held accountable for anything, and they are regularly the victims in their own lives. It's nearly impossible to get people like this to "own" their behavior or admit to making mistakes.

The ability to be self-reflective and truly accountable for their own actions is one of the most precious gifts that parents can give children. Young as she was, Anne Frank understood this well when she wrote, "Parents can only give good advice or put them on the right paths, but the final forming of a person's character lies in their own hands."

Every year on Yom Kippur we are reminded to acknowledge the mistakes we have made during the past year, repent, and commit ourselves to changing in the future. The wisdom of Maimonides offers everyday guidance to help us all understand, reflect on, and change our behavior. He explains, "Repentance is completed when an opportunity to commit one's original transgression again arises but one doesn't and repents instead" (*Mishneh Torah*, Hilchot Teshuvah 2:1).

Maimonides lays out in his book *Mishneh Torah* (Hilchot Teshuvah 2:2) three steps toward changing problematic behavior. In English, each of these stages begins with the letter *R*: recognize, remorse, and resolve.

1. *Recognize the problem.* Maimonides explains that a person should "abandon the sin and remove it from his [or her] thoughts," acknowledging behavior that was unacceptable. If we aren't aware that anything is wrong, we won't do anything to change our behavior.

2. *Feel remorse about the problem.* In Maimonides' words, the person "should regret the past." In order to change our ways, we must regret our actions.

3. *Resolve to solve the problem.* As Maimonides says, a person must "resign in his heart never to commit it again." We must not only determine in our minds to change our behavior but also have a concrete plan for doing so, so the next time we are tempted, we won't make the same mistake.

While these three steps can be incredibly helpful in our own lives, we can also use them to teach our children how to improve their attitudes toward mistakes they have made. Let's look more closely at how we can do this, step by step, as parents.

RECOGNIZE THE PROBLEM

Because young children can be very literal, it helps when parents use very clear language to explain why a specific behavior is unacceptable. However, with kids of any age, it can be risky to assume they know what they've done wrong. Listen carefully to gauge how much they understand. Sometimes kids will know their behavior is problematic, but sometimes they won't.

Of course, sometimes they might know but think they can get away with it. If you catch your child taking a candy bar from a store, he may know in theory that it's wrong to steal. But depending on his age, level of development, and sophistication, he may not understand that what he did was theft. A young child may just see the candy bar, want it, and take it. If he's a little older, he may justify it to himself, telling himself it's just a small thing that nobody will miss, or that he deserves it and it's his parents' fault for not buying it for him.

Think of something your child has done wrong recently. How could you reframe it in a non-accusatory way?

Regardless of how much your child understands, it is almost always fruitless to ask the question, "Why did you do that?" Instead, the first step is to stay as calm as we can and keep *our* emotions under control. Problem solving while angry is rarely effective. When our thoughts are clouded by intense feelings, it's nearly impossible to see things clearly, and we're likely to regret any action we took in the heat of the moment.

State the issue at hand in a way that is not accusatory or judgmental. We might say something like, "I see that you hit your brother," instead of, "You are so mean to your brother; what's wrong with you?" Keeping cool and avoiding accusations and hurtful labels will help our children feel more comfortable admitting that they did something wrong. The goal here is to get the child to acknowledge it so we can help them change. And we're all more likely to acknowledge a problem when we're not on the defensive.

Reassure your child that everybody makes mistakes, and defuse any embarrassment by explaining that this is how people learn. Explain that you're going to find ways together to fix this mistake and make sure it doesn't happen again.

Of course, handling a situation this way doesn't guarantee that your child will admit that he did anything wrong. We all know how easy it is to go around in circles with "no, I didn't—yes, you did—no, I didn't" scenarios. Don't keep arguing in circles.

Just let him talk and listen respectfully. As we mentioned in chapter one, listening to children doesn't mean that you're agreeing. Sometimes, once they feel heard and somewhat validated, they'll be more willing to cooperate to solve the problem (which is the ultimate goal here). That takes us to the next of our three *R*'s—remorse.

Feel Remorse

Once we've gotten the problem out in the open, the next step is to help the child sincerely feel sorry about the behavior. Having the integrity to feel sorry and show honest remorse or regret is a very important step toward change. Remorse or regret can be broken down into three components:

1. Understanding how our actions hurt other individuals

2. Understanding how our actions hurt our community

3. Understanding how our actions hurt us

As with recognition, remorse is best accomplished through calm, matter-of-fact, non-accusatory discussion. Lectures, guilt trips, and angry rants won't make a child feel genuine regret. Instead, they might make children feel threatened or hopelessly negative about themselves, and the goal here isn't just to make them feel bad.

In order to encourage remorse, it's helpful to gently point out to children the negative effects of their behavior on themselves, others, and the community. Here's how to bring this up:

- When you hit someone, it hurts them. (affects others)

- When you talk meanly to people, they won't want to play with you. (affects self)

- When you are too loud in the lunchroom, the whole cafeteria loses talking privileges and people will be annoyed at you. (affects community and self)

- When you leave your bike too close to the street, it can get hit by a car. (affects self—ruined bike; affects others—damage to a person's car)

Try This! BEANBAG REMORSE

A perfect throw? In his book *Building Jewish Life: Rosh Ha-Shanah & Yom Kippur*, Joel Lurie Grishaver suggests having kids toss three beanbags into a wastebasket way over on the other side of the room. Any child who can't do it is out. Of course, most kids can't get all three beanbags in on the first try. But if we let them take back any beanbags that miss, with a chance to toss them again, they're sure to get them all in eventually. This is how Judaism views teshuvah and sincere remorse—we all make mistakes, all the time, but teshuvah gives us a chance to take back our mistakes and toss those beanbags again. What a positive message to share with our children—that feeling bad about mistakes is an important step toward becoming the better people we know they can be!

- When you cheat on schoolwork, you might get caught and get a failing grade, and you might get behind in your work. (affects self)

- When you cheat in a game, no one will want to play with you, and it's not fair to others. (affects self and others)

Saying "I'm sorry" is not the same as feeling remorse or regret. Most three-year-olds can be taught to say they're sorry. But does the child really understand what he or she did and how it negatively affected him- or herself or others in a way that will change the child's future behavior? Children can definitely absorb this as they develop and grow.

By age seven or eight, children can usually connect their actions to an effect on another person. However, they don't internalize this concept fully until much later, perhaps until their teens.

So be prepared for a lot of repetition and explanation as problems arise. In order to truly help a child change a negative behavior, we need to take the time to explain and guide the child at his or her level. Then, we must follow through in a way that will keep the child accountable for his or her actions. In the incident with the stolen candy bar above, we could go with the child to return the candy bar and apologize to the cashier (decide in advance what you'll do if the cashier tells him he can keep it in return for his honesty; this really does happen!).

When we ask our kids to experience and express remorse, we are showing them that we're confident that they can learn from what happened and do better next time. Then, they can take that learning and apply their problem-solving skills.

RESOLVE TO SOLVE THE PROBLEM

The final stage in successfully changing behavior is to identify the specific behavior we want to change and plan ahead of time what we will do the next time the situation arises. When we have a predetermined strategy in place, we are much more likely to achieve the behavior we hope to develop. When applying this idea to our children, we have to involve them in developing the plan of action. Including them in figuring out a solution acknowledges that their contribution is important and empowers them to steer themselves toward responsible behavior.

Once our child has returned the candy bar, and any residual anger or embarrassment over the incident has cooled, it can be helpful to sit down with the child and talk about what's going to happen next time he's in a store and wants something. You can acknowledge how tempting it must have been to take it and that he might be tempted again next time. Depending, again, on his age and sophistication, you can brainstorm action plans, which could range from your buying a treat once a week to an older child doing special tasks to save up money for candy. You can also point out that he could have asked you to buy it for him, being sure to explain that you will not always say "yes" to everything he wants while you're in a store together.

When we involve kids in taking responsibility for this third *R*, deciding how change can, should, and will happen, they will more willingly participate in finding a solution that works for everyone. They also will be able to take credit for any positive outcomes that may result. Of course, it may take multiple attempts or strategies to get a satisfactory end result. But in this way, your child will become accountable for his or her own actions—and gain some problem-solving techniques in the process.

Beyond creating a workable action plan, a major part of the resolution R is to make amends for any wrong that's been done. This refers to longer-term consequences, not a short-term, urgent situation. If a child's friend is hurt and needs help, obviously, that should be taken care of immediately before thoughts of any other steps enter the picture. However, before the situation can be fully resolved, Maimonides writes, the person who's been wronged must be "appeased" (*Mishneh Torah*, Hilchot Teshuvah 2:9). He writes that we must go to great lengths to attain forgiveness from another person, but also cautions the one who's been wronged, saying, "It is forbidden for a person to be cruel and refuse to be appeased" (2:10). This, too, emphasizes the importance of seeking and granting forgiveness, actions that stem from empathy for one another.

Our children need to know that when their actions lead to another person's suffering, pain, or loss, they have a responsibility to make it up to that person. Here are some ways children can learn to make amends:

- If a child breaks or loses a toy belonging to another child, she can give something of her own or use her allowance to replace it.

- If a rough game does damage to a neighbor's property, a child can help the neighbor fix the damage or work off the debt by doing some yard work (even if you've already compensated the neighbor in any way required by law).

- If a child has taken something that's impossible to return, see if it can be donated so someone else can enjoy it instead.

We can also help our kids by talking things through and offering them constructive ways to avoid pitfalls in the future:

- If a game looks like it is getting rough, find another game to play.

- When playing in a place where something can get broken or destroyed, move to another location.

- If there's not enough time to do schoolwork, let parents know so you can plan together.

- Pick a special parking place for the bicycle.

- If it's hard to remember to bring homework to school, pin a note inside the backpack asking them to check if there's homework inside.

As these examples show, this "resolution" step is not the same as punishment. It's simply teaching our kids to realize the impact that they have on others, to see how their actions have consequences, and to recognize the importance of making amends. Even if the harm was not intentional, we can still help our children by encouraging them to be a part of the process of resolving the problem. In fact, there may be no skill more useful than problem solving to help our children navigate future challenges.

Practice Problem Solving

King Solomon sure knew how to solve a problem. When two women each claimed that a certain baby was hers, King Solomon suggested that they divide the baby in half. Of course he knew that the real mother would choose to give up her baby rather than have him die, and that is exactly what happened (1 Kings 3:16–27).

Problems are inevitable whenever people live together. So we need to equip our children to solve problems that are both minor and more significant.

Problem solving is actually a very learnable skill, and one we can apply in a variety of situations. Problem solving benefits us not only with our family, but also at work, with friends, and in many other situations. In our children's lives, they can use problem solving at school, with friends, with siblings, and to deal with other worries that come as a part of growing up.

As adults, we already use problem solving to help address our frustrations head-on and keep our homes peaceful and nurturing, the kind of refuge that we all need from the frantic outside world.

Before we can start modeling these skills for our children, let's begin by understanding the process of problem solving. Here is an eight-step sequence that can help you and that you can teach your children:

1. Listen to your feelings. Identify inner signs of anger or anxiety. Collect yourself and prepare to problem solve.

2. State the problem as you see it, either aloud or in writing. This will help you focus on your objective or goal—what you want to have happen.

3. Brainstorm solutions. Think of different things you (not others) could do to reach this goal. Think of several solutions. Research has shown that the more effective ideas usually are not the first ones that come to mind.

4. Evaluate solutions. Think through which solution would best help you achieve your goal.

5. Choose the idea/solution you think will work best.

6. Plan or think through the steps that are needed to carry out this idea. Try to foresee obstacles that might hinder your efforts and consider how you might handle them.

7. Try it out. If your solution works, great! If not, try another idea, always keeping your goal in mind.

8. Think through what you can do to avoid this problem in the future.

Though these steps apply in most cases, problem solving is a personal process that we tailor to fit our own individual needs. So what works for another person may not be the right thing for you, and what you consider to be the best response in a particular situation may not work for someone else.

Let's take a look at two specific, practical examples of how to follow these steps with our families: laundry and extracurricular activities.

Problem #1: Laundry piling up

This is a common scenario, even with the youngest kids.

1. Listen to your feelings:

   "I'm feeling very stressed and overwhelmed because dirty laundry is piled up everywhere."

2. State the problem:

   "There is more laundry than I have the energy to do. I would like to get the clothes clean, but I also need to relax a little tonight."

3. Brainstorm solutions:

   "I just won't do the laundry."

   "I could sort through the dirty clothes and run just one load."

   "I could wash a couple of loads and have the kids fold the clean clothes themselves."

   "I could wait until the children are in bed and stay up late to get it all done."

4. Evaluate solutions:

   "I can't leave the laundry because more dirty clothes are going to pile up tomorrow."

   "If I do just one load, it will help, but I will still have more to do tomorrow."

   "I don't have to do everything myself because the kids could do some of the work."

   "Staying up late to do laundry is difficult. I have to be up early in the morning because tomorrow is a busy day."

5. Choose a solution:

   "This isn't a good day for me to stay up late to get the whole job done, but I have enough energy to do one load."

6. Plan:

   "I'll get the wash started and let the kids know that they're going to put their clothes away when it's done. Then tomorrow I'll start the remaining clothes a little earlier and have the kids help fold the laundry. "

Problem #2: The stress of extracurricular activities

Between home and work responsibilities, school requirements, and extracurricular activities, our lives feel hectic, overscheduled, and even chaotic at times. We want our kids to have educational, social, and entertaining experiences outside of school, but juggling all these activities can be overwhelming and often leads to time-management conflicts. Using problem-solving steps that we are modeling ourselves, we can help guide our children toward a solution that works for the entire family.

1. Listen to your feelings:

   "My head is about to explode trying to figure out how to get my son to soccer practice when my daughter needs to be at dance across town. And tomorrow is the same thing; two different activities in two different places."

2. State the problem:

   "I cannot be in two places at one time."
   "It is overwhelming to run from place to place most nights of the week for kids' activities."

*"I'm having trouble keeping up with the house and get-
ting dinner on the table when I'm running around every
night."*

*"The kids are too tired in the morning and need more sleep
and downtime during the week."*

3. Brainstorm solutions:

    *"I could talk to some of the other parents who live close by
    about carpooling."*

    *"We can have them drop out of their extracurricular activi-
    ties for now."*

    *"I'll try to get all the housework done before work or on the
    weekends, and we'll order pizza or have takeout for dinner
    during the week."*

    *"We could cut back on activities and allow each child just
    one weeknight activity each."*

    *"We could find out if there are any activities they'd enjoy
    closer to home so we're not driving all over town."*

4. Evaluate solutions:

    *"I don't want the kids to miss out on extracurricular
    activities, and it wouldn't be fair to pull children out of
    their activities."*

    *"The kids do not need to be involved in every single activity
    every single semester."*

    *"I need help because doing it on my own isn't working. I
    cannot keep this schedule up."*

    *"We can sit down and prioritize the activities that are most
    important to each of them and cut back on the ones that
    are less important."*

"I can check with parents I know in each activity to see if we could alternate days to carpool so that I don't need to be in two places at once."

5. Choose a solution:

"Extracurricular interests are important for my children's development, but my children don't need to do everything."

6. Plan:

"So tomorrow we'll sit down and prioritize what each child wants to do. Then we'll cut back on each child's weeknight activities, and I will check on possible carpools."

Because every family is different, this process can be tailored to fit the specific needs and interests of each family. It is important to take the time to build problem-solving skills and to take the necessary steps when issues come up, while trying to foresee any possible obstacles.

These deliberate actions also send a very important message to our children: that as parents, we persevere and take whatever steps are needed to confront and overcome conflicts.

Involving kids in this process will give them more confidence in the outcome because they were part of solving the problem. They'll be much more likely to agree to the solution and own it because they took an active role in working it out. They'll know their voice was heard and they will feel validated enough to at least try to make the agreed-upon solution work.

Walking through the deliberate steps of problem solving is essential in effective parenting. It is through the repetition of this process with our children and talking through their thoughts about how to proceed that we build our children's capacity to resolve their own problems with friends and with each other. A classic Jewish joke shows this principle at work:

> *Mom:* Sidney, it's time to get up and go to school.
>
> *Sidney:* Mom, I don't want to.
>
> *Mom:* Sidney, you have to; you're going to be late.
>
> *Sidney:* It's too difficult! I don't want to deal with the teachers, and the kids all hate me.
>
> *Mom:* Sidney, you have to get up. You're the principal!

Our children's ability to think through and solve their own conflicts will benefit them personally, socially, and professionally for the rest of their lives. When they acquire these skills, it also lifts some of the burden off of us as parents, as—all joking aside— we cannot solve our children's problems throughout their lives.

Wrap-Up

We started this chapter by explaining the significance and influence that our home environment has on our kids. It is at home that we first model for our children the essential characteristic of responsibility. Our goal in doing this is to mold our kids into productive, contributing, dependable people. Responsibility is a key to their success in life now (in school, sports, and other areas) and in their becoming effective, thriving adults with successful relationships and careers.

Responsibility is a crucial component of the continuity of the Jewish people: producing responsible community members with unlimited potential to use their voices and actions to leave a positive, beautiful mark on this world. So as we wrap up this chapter, let's look to the future with joy and wonder at the tremendous opportunities that lie before our children.

From Oy to Joy!

You'll know that you are moving from oy to joy when your child...

- admits to taking your wavy scrapbooking scissors without permission, saving you the "third degree."

- clears the table willingly (or even with enthusiasm).

- shows concern for the state of the planet and takes initiative to do more at home.

- starts making her own plan to avoid being near the kids at school who provoke her into fighting.

spark Motivation

"When you perform a mitzvah, do not concern yourself
with the reward you may receive. Make yourself like a tightrope
walker in a carnival. If he thinks of the rewards he may receive,
he surely will lose his footing and fall."
—*Chasidic teaching*

"Motivation is when your dreams put on work clothes."
—*Benjamin Franklin*

■ ■ ■

*When six-year-old Ryan Hreljac's first-grade teacher told his class
that children in Africa had to walk miles to get clean water from
distant wells, Ryan decided to do something about it. He per-
suaded his parents to pay him to do extra jobs around the house
so he could save up the seventy dollars he thought it would cost
to build a well in Africa. Even when he realized it would take
two thousand dollars, he persevered and did even more chores.*

He also expanded his fundraising efforts, which included speaking publicly about what he was trying to do. And what a success story it has been! Since 1998, the Ryan's Well Foundation (www.ryanswell.ca) has improved the lives of over one million people through its clean water projects.

■ ■ ■

Ryan Hreljac started raising money for his project at just six years of age, through his own initiative and with his parents' help and support. What can we do in our own homes to help our children become self-motivated in this kind of way?

Motivating children can often seem like an insurmountable task. Helping them shift from merely obeying instructions (to clean their rooms, make their beds, pick up after themselves) to being driven from within is a big job; it takes even more to start an international project like Ryan's. How can we help our kids act on their own initiative without prodding or bribery? Every aspect of our children's future is tied to their ability to motivate themselves to keep moving forward.

Judaism stresses action—doing the right thing—for its own sake. That is an important message we can share with our children. *No discussing it endlessly. It's simply the right thing to do.* And by practicing and doing the things that need to be done, children can start to internalize the value of their actions/behavior. Our children may not initially appreciate doing certain tasks, but they can begin to appreciate the importance of their contribution, especially when it comes to helping with everyday jobs at home and being a part of a family team. Jewish teachings also stress humility. We do the right thing not because we will get recognition or a prize, but because that is the proper way to behave. Our history is filled with scores of stories of humble people who reached out to others and repaired the world anonymously. Not only did they not *expect* recognition, they didn't *want* it.

One famous Jewish legend tells of Yossele the miser. He was the richest man in his village, but scorned by all for his stinginess and refusal to contribute anything when tzedakah collectors came calling. He was so despised that when he died, the villagers only grudgingly buried him in the back of the cemetery in the section reserved for paupers. However, a few days later, strange things started happening in the village. One poor person after another showed up at the rabbi's doorstep begging for money. He discovered that each had been receiving a weekly allowance, but none knew where it had come from. The rabbi immediately realized how greatly Yossele had been wronged. The townspeople gathered at Yossele's graveside to beg for his forgiveness. On the tombstone, which had read "Yossele the Miser," the townspeople added the word *HaTzaddik*—the Righteous One.

This tale, related for hundreds of years, underscores the importance in Judaism of taking initiative and doing the right thing—in this case, serving the community humbly even if we're not rewarded for it, in the same spirit that Ryan Hreljac undertook his project.

What can we bring into our homes to help inspire this kind of motivation in our kids? In this chapter, we will dive into four ways we can help bring this about.

- Let go

- Build competence and confidence

- Create connections

- Encourage effort and accomplishment

As with most character attributes, building motivation is like building up muscle strength. The more our kids "work out," the stronger they'll become. Even during periods of hardship, our kids must be able to move forward and motivate themselves.

Let Go

As parents, it can be difficult to let go so our children can act on their own, especially when we see them struggling or feel like we could help them do it better. As we saw in chapter four, the Talmud instructs parents to teach their children to swim. How does this lesson help us learn to let go? It teaches us that children must be taught survival skills so that, ultimately, they can survive independently from us.

This process can also be tough on us. We may feel like we're losing control, closeness, or importance in our kids' lives. The babies that we nurtured, coddled, and protected don't need us in the same way. This is hard, but it's a necessity of letting children take responsibility for their own lives.

Rest assured: our kids will always need us, in different ways at different stages. So letting go so they can mature into the next natural stage of our relationship with them is actually the best way to stay connected.

As children learn to manage their lives and accomplish goals without us—picking out their own clothes, completing a school assignment, remembering to practice piano, negotiating friendships, and, later in life, waking up to get to school, and getting and keeping a job—they'll still need our advice, support, and companionship. But none of this will happen easily if we don't start letting go so they'll learn to function independently.

Letting kids work things out for themselves motivates them to strive and overcome obstacles. It's the process that counts. Accomplishing something on our own is a wonderful feeling, a joy that we definitely want our children to experience! Let's consider some basic steps that will help us encourage our children on their journey toward self-motivation:

- *Start today.* At almost any age or stage, our kids can learn elements of self-sufficiency. Even as toddlers, their independent play is a healthy part of development. So don't put it off until your kids are "old enough."

- *Let them figure it out.* Don't immediately jump in and fix whatever they're working on. As tough as it might be, bite your tongue. Let them do it the way they think they should. Sure, they won't do the job the way we could: beds might be lumpy, clothes might be mismatched, and their form on the field might not be stellar. Perfection is not the point here; we're working toward motivation and independence.

- *Encourage them to keep trying, even if it's in baby steps.* With each tiny success, our kids will learn the positive feelings that come with achievement. Letting them work things out will give them the confidence to take bigger steps on their own.

- *Don't give in to whining or bad attitudes.* If we surrender and take over when our kids complain, how will they ever learn motivation? As adults, a bad attitude won't help them, so don't let them benefit from it now either.

- *Express appreciation.* Your positive feedback will encourage repetition of the behavior, and their efforts will get better with time.

- *Give them some freedom to choose.* Kids might not get to decide where the next family vacation will be, but they can suggest some vacation activities. Kids should not decide whether the family will collect tzedakah (donations for charity), but they can help decide where the money will go. When kids see that their choices make a real difference, they'll be even more motivated next time.

Build Competence and Confidence

Judaism places great importance on study, for both children and adults. The Torah tells parents to spend a lot of time teaching the laws and commandments because these are guides for living: "Teach them to your children, talking about them while sitting

Try This! BUILDING COMPETENCE

Join in an annual fundraising activity taking place in your community to support a cause that you choose together. This could be medical (heart, stroke, cancer), Jewish (a school, Israel), or anything else that aligns with your family's values. Encourage each child to collect pledges as independently as possible. For young kids, you can accompany them to friends' doors or place phone calls to relatives for them, but try to have your children say a word or two if possible about the cause. Their "pitch" will become smoother the more they repeat it, making them more confident each time they say it. Older kids can be more active, under your supervision. Copy or scan each child's pledge sheet before you turn it in to organizers so he or she can contact the same individuals again the following year. Make it a contest—kids don't have to beat each other, but let them try to beat the amount they raised the previous year, even by a little. Everybody wins!

in your house, walking on the road, or when you are about to lie down or get up" (Deuteronomy 11:19). Even before the first century, Jewish sources talked about the necessity of establishing elementary schools to teach young children.

Modern psychology backs this up: knowledge leads to competence, and competence leads to confidence. Competence, confidence, and motivation feed off one another in a virtuous cycle, which is the exact opposite of a vicious cycle. The more competent children become, the more their confidence grows. And as their confidence goes up, the drive to become more capable and skilled increases. They are then more motivated to take on responsibilities that will increase their competence and confidence. We've seen this cycle at work in a wide range of children, regardless of their innate abilities.

Most of the time, as parents, we think we know what is best for our kids. But we need to think about and pay attention to what *our kids* think might be best for them.

Nine-year-old Anna tried every trick in the book to avoid practicing the violin—her hand hurt, it was too noisy in the house, she was too tired. It was a constant battle for her parents. Then, her violin teacher suggested that she try the guitar instead. Anna discovered that she loved being able to play songs people knew so they could sing along. She started to feel like a rock star and loved singing along loudly. And guess what? No more battles with her parents over practice time.

The question for us is, how can we start this virtuous cycle of competence leading to confidence leading to motivation, and how can we provide a balance between offering the support that our children need and giving them independence?

Here are a few simple ways we can foster attitudes that instill confidence and competence:

- *Set realistic and manageable goals.* Competence comes from meeting challenges that are neither too easy nor too difficult, but just enough of a stretch that, with some effort, success is possible. In the story of Goldilocks and the three bears, Goldilocks was looking for the porridge, the chair, and the bed that were "juuust right." So, too, we must offer the ideal level of challenge to our children.

● *Keep our own feelings and expectations in check.* Whether our expectations are unrealistically high or depressingly low, they can strip away children's motivation. Children will feel overwhelmed, frustrated, or incapable—or they won't feel challenged enough to even bother. Communicating that we expect and appreciate their involvement in a task—at an age-appropriate level—will help them feel competent and capable of contributing.

● *Encourage children's questions.* One of our children once asked, "If God is everywhere, is he up my nose?" Not a bad theological question for a four-year-old! Brace yourself for questions that might catch you off guard. It's okay if you don't have a perfect response ready. Our children have to know that asking questions is good, even when a question may seem silly to us. This will reinforce for them that their ideas matter and will build self-motivation when they see that they, too, can contribute. Questioning is a huge part of the Jewish tradition: Moses even questioned God. This means allowing kids to ask (respectfully and within reason) about our choices as parents and why we have made them.

● *Express disapproval carefully and tactfully.* What child never does anything her parents disapprove of? But there are positive ways even to express our disapproval.

Criticism and sarcasm undermine motivation because children feel rejected; gentle correction and guidance enhance motivation, reinforcing the idea that we believe in them and their ability to improve. Instead of "That was a foolish thing to do," try "How could you make a better decision next time?"

- *Provide instructive guidance.* Steer them toward opportunities that are likely to build feelings of competence and confidence, engaging them in a way that they can see the real value and impact of their work. Jewish tradition requires us, as adults, to provide instruction and guidance. The Torah tells us not simply to *teach* children Jewish laws and customs but to "teach them diligently" (Deuteronomy 6:7). Prudent, hands-on involvement by parents is a good thing and—used carefully—helps build our children's self-motivation.

What are each of your children's strengths? How could you encourage each of them in these areas?

Create Connections

Community is a central Jewish concept. There are certain prayers we can say only with a minyan (a minimum of ten Jewish adults). We are warned not to separate ourselves from the community (*Pirkei Avot* 2:5) and that we are all responsible for each other (Talmud, *Shevu'ot* 39a). In chapter two, we explored the way that some of our communal traditions and celebrations have held the Jewish people together for thousands of years. We thrive when we feel part of a greater whole, and celebrations give us security through a sense of belonging, both to our family and to our community. Collective interaction and shared values help us accomplish communal goals. Relationships matter. Belonging matters.

Being connected to others feels good, but beyond that, connection and collaboration increase motivation and responsibility. The familiar saying "A chain is only as strong as its weakest link" reminds us that when people are counting on us to help accomplish a goal, the entire group's efforts will be undermined if we fail. Being connected makes us accountable; we don't want to disappoint other people.

Working side by side with others also provides a support system that affirms and motivates us all. Connections are so valuable that it's worth finding ways to help our children create them as well. Here are a few ideas for encouraging our children to create and strengthen connections:

- *Establish traditions.* Find, adapt, or create customs or traditions to bring immediate and extended family members or friends together regularly. This might be celebrations of holidays, Shabbat, or a life-cycle celebration. The reason for getting together doesn't matter as much as its regularity. Feeling connected truly begins with family.

- *Get involved.* Encourage children to get involved through volunteering with civic groups or political organizations to teach them the importance and value of being part of a wider community.

- *Create varied experiences.* Like adults, kids have very different tastes and personalities. As we work toward creating connections for our kids, provide a wide array of experiences so that they can discover interests that they find most motivating. For some, it might be a hands-on group project like building a sukkah at a local seniors' residence; for others, quieter one-on-one interactions, like visiting an older person, may be more appealing.

Try This! CREATING CONNECTIONS

Gather a few families and help organize a community potluck Shabbat or festival meal. Make up a chart of dishes, supplies, and responsibilities, making sure that not too much falls on any one person. You're doing this, in part, to demonstrate to children that "many hands make light work," with everybody participating relying on everybody else for food and other needs. Let your kids sign up for tasks as well. Children as young as five or six can set or clear tables or even sweep up afterward, while older children can plan games and activities (such as face painting at a Purim celebration, or a Shabbat sing-along or play) to help keep younger kids entertained. Keep it light and fun; the goal is community and companionship, not a perfect, restaurant-quality meal.

- *Keep it fresh and full of energy.* Don't fall into a duty-bound mentality that can work against actually motivating children. Occasionally substituting new activities can add energy and help keep kids connecting.

- *Show interest and enthusiasm.* Never take children's motivation for granted; try to mirror their excitement as they take on new initiatives and create connections on their own.

- *Encourage children to reflect on their experiences*, and help them talk through any anxiety or concerns that may come up. Perhaps a child who normally excels in everything has started taking Judo and he's worried that although he likes the class, he's not very good at it. Listen as he talks it through and don't rush to either suggest that he quit or force him to stay.

Encourage Effort and Accomplishment

Never underestimate the impact that our own attitudes and feelings have on our kids' motivation. Remember, people live up or down to the expectations placed upon them. The messages we send to our children about our belief in them and their abilities have a big impact.

Knowing someone else is confident that we'll succeed is a powerfully motivating feeling. Messages to our children like "I know

Can you think of something your child has done in the last few days that's taken an extraordinary effort?

this is challenging, but I think you can handle it" or "I'm sure you'll find a good way to take care of it" convey our confidence in their abilities. Likewise, statements such as "You'll do the right thing" or "I'm sure you'll behave appropriately" express confidence in their character. Words of encouragement are powerful tools in propelling our children in the direction of productive and worthy behavior.

Jewish tradition teaches that every person has the capacity to choose right or wrong; when we choose to do what's morally right, we feel good about our choice and about ourselves, an intrinsic reward that becomes a motivating factor next time.

Performing mitzvot is an example of this. Ideally, we would do them out of love and responsibility, and not because we expect a reward: "The reward for a mitzvah is the mitzvah itself" (*Pirkei Avot* 4:2). Of course, at times, it's also nice if external recognition further encourages the behavior. But that is not the primary reason for doing a mitzvah in the first place.

As we encourage our children to work toward their goals, let's look at two common encouragement strategies, reward and praise.

REWARDING OUR CHILDREN

When our kids are young, using incentives or rewards so they'll behave in a certain way may seem to be effective. As most parents have realized, offering a small reward to a toddler or preschooler can help steer or redirect the child so that we don't have to launch a full-on battle of the wills.

We should also start taking a global view, in which rewards are a tool to help our children establish the *habit* of doing the right thing. Rewards can create positive feelings around the behavior we want and, used strategically, can reinforce behavior we want to see the child engage in on his or her own.

However, since over-rewarding can actually demotivate children, who quickly learn to refuse to take any action until you offer a reward, we ultimately want to shift kids away from rewards. Instead, we must try to steer them toward understanding the effects of their actions on others, though this understanding often takes a lot of explaining and reinforcing on our part. Relying on rewards too often or for too long makes the prize itself the incentive, instead of the satisfying feeling of achievement, contribution, or simply pleasing someone special.

The British television series *Child of our Time* conducted an interesting experiment with some children. They asked a group of five-year-olds who liked drawing to divide into two groups. One group was asked to draw a picture about whatever they wished. The second group was asked to do the same, but they were also offered a small reward—a toy—for their work on the picture. In *The Guardian*, Tessa Livingstone describes what they discovered:

> *At the end of five minutes we collected the pictures and handed over the promised reward to the second group. What happened next was startling. The rewarded children*

talked, threw paper balls and wandered about the room. They wanted to do anything but draw. But the children who had no reward settled back to drawing as though their lives depended on it.

Instead of offering rewards to our children to motivate them to do the right thing, we can lead them in that direction through affirmation and encouragement. We can verbally build our children up and then set appropriate expectations so they learn to do the right thing without being rewarded. We can assign tasks in a positive, encouraging way by saying, "I expect that you'll pick up your toys before supper," "I look forward to seeing what clothes you'll pick out for school tomorrow," "I expect that you'll take out the trash before seven," or "I'm sure that you're going to allow enough time to practice so you're prepared to do your best at your recital."

Once our children are adults, they will know very well that their behavior won't always be rewarded. Sure, some aspects of adult life seem reward based, like getting paid for doing our jobs or winning prizes for excellence in various fields. But as adults, we must also fulfill many responsibilities without external rewards: maintaining our homes, feeding and clothing our families, taking care of extended family, paying bills, and keeping up our cars. Living a responsible, productive life must be sufficient motivation in and of itself.

We can teach kids the value of embracing the intrinsic rewards that come from helping others. Bringing food to a homeless shelter and knowing the recipients will have a good meal as a result can be a reward in itself. Donating books they no longer need to a school that will distribute them to other children can give kids a wonderful feeling inside. However you do it, helping others can make many actions feel more special. Not only are we sharing what we have with others, we also feel the satisfaction and internal joy of contributing to the greater good.

We saw earlier in this chapter that the reward for a mitzvah is the mitzvah itself. Educator and author Robyn R. Jackson has arrived at the same conclusion, as she wrote in her book *Never Work Harder Than Your Students and Other Principles of Great Teaching*: "Rather than rewarding students for doing their job, we should help them celebrate a job well done. It's a subtle shift but an important one. Celebrating their success leaves the onus where it should be, with the student." We must ultimately teach our children that the reward should never become the goal.

Praising Our Children

Encouragement is important, and we all need to receive it. Both encouragement (in the form of support, hope, and motivation) and praise (the expression of approval or admiration) can go a long way toward motivating our kids to accomplish a task or achieve a goal. But both are best used wisely, intentionally, and with care.

The self-esteem movement of the 1980s aimed to increase children's sense of self-worth by highlighting their accomplishments. This was based on the belief that low self-esteem reduced motivation, decreased productivity, and increased social problems. For years, parents were encouraged to tell children how smart they were, how beautiful or handsome they were, how athletic and talented they were, all so that their self-esteem would be high and they would feel good about themselves. Children received trophies or medals simply for showing up at a track meet or soccer game.

Our sages seem to have known better. *Eishet Chayil* (Woman of Valor), from the Book of Proverbs (Proverbs 31:10–31), read at the Shabbat table, praises the virtuous woman for her *deeds*, not her *words*. Her actions, which have built up and supported her family and the community, are what bring her true appreciation and praise in life. Recognition follows action, not the other way around.

Of course, we should always communicate to our children that we value and love them. But that is not the same as throwing praise at them, which can backfire when it's overdone or without merit. When children are praised excessively or without merit...

- They can develop an overinflated view of themselves and their importance. This can lead to big letdowns when they don't get that same praise from others.

- They will only do things that they get praised for. If there's no praise, why bother? Praise "junkies" can't function without massive amounts of praise.

- They won't learn to act simply because it's the right thing to do or because it might benefit someone else.

- They could start to manipulate their efforts based on the praise they receive. More praise and accolades equal more effort.

- Their self-esteem could stem only from the praise they receive. If a coach or a teacher doesn't offer the praise they need to feel good, their emotions will be negatively affected.

Developmental psychologist Carol S. Dweck studied the effects of praise on hundreds of students, mostly early adolescents. "We first gave each student a set of ten fairly difficult problems from a nonverbal IQ test," she writes in her book *Mindset: The New Psychology of Success.*

> *They mostly did pretty well on these, and when they finished we praised them. We praised some of the students for their ability. They were told, "Wow, you got [say] eight right. That's a really good score. You must be smart at this."...We praised other students for their effort: "Wow, you got [say] eight right. That's a really good score. You must have worked really hard." They were not made to feel they had some special gift; they were praised for doing what it takes to succeed. Both groups were exactly the same to begin with. But right after the praise, they began to differ. When we gave them [the ability-praised students] a choice, they rejected a challenging new task they could learn from. They didn't want to do anything that could expose their flaws and call into question their talent....In contrast, when students were praised for effort, 90 percent of them wanted the challenging new task that they could learn from.*

Dweck then gave all the students some difficult problems. She found that the effort-praised students still loved the problems, while those praised for ability said that the problems weren't fun anymore. Moreover, those students did worse on the problems, while their effort-praised peers kept improving.

Praising children for their effort can inspire them, because they know they have control over effort. However, praising them for their *ability* might discourage them, because they may not feel they have the ability to succeed.

We often are tempted to praise our children to make them feel better when things aren't going well. This is where the subtle difference between encouragement and praise comes in. We definitely want to *encourage* our children, especially during a struggle, since this can keep their spirits up and give them what they need to persevere despite obstacles.

What if you have a child on the field whose throwing ability is mediocre? Instead of falsely praising her ball-throwing skill, encourage her to keep trying or to give it her best. Children usually have a pretty good idea of how their efforts stack up to reality. So if they know that you aren't being completely truthful about their performance, praise can actually make them feel worse. Unrealistic praise is discouraging and demotivating to people of all ages.

How can we let our kids know that we are proud of them and their efforts without getting them hooked on our praise? Here are some ways that we can draw out their best efforts; our kids will feel good about themselves and encouraged to keep trying.

- *Praise genuine effort.* As Carol Dweck found, there's a big difference between praising children for their ability ("You must be really smart!") and praising them for their effort ("You must have worked really hard!"). When praised for ability, children tend to focus more on "looking" smart; when praised for effort, they tend to focus more on successfully accomplishing a task.

- *Cool it—don't go overboard.* Our children need positive feedback when they are doing something right and benefit from encouragement for both hard work and good results. But don't exaggerate praise so it becomes more flattery than truth. Rashi, one of greatest commentators on the Bible and Talmud, who lived in eleventh-century France, said, "It is forbidden to praise another excessively" (Talmud, *Arachin* 16a). Try saying something like "That's an excellent grade on the test, you must be proud," instead of "You're so smart, getting that grade. You're my little genius."

- *Stick to the issue at hand.* We don't need to praise our child's entire personality or character in one big statement. If our children do a good job cleaning their rooms, then saying, "The room looks very neat" is appropriate. Over-the-top (and unearned) praise might be, "You're the neatest child in the world." We love making our children feel good, but focusing our praise on a child's specific behavior is most helpful in the long run.

- *Choose what you praise.* The actions we choose to praise let our children know what's important to us. It's easy to notice the bigger things, like good grades or sports success. But try to keep a lookout for and praise any new initiatives—great or small—like taking time to study for an exam (and what that says about a child's motivation to get good grades), being a mensch and helping a disabled person, or taking the initiative to help out a younger child who needs it.

By describing the specifics of what they are doing, we give children the feedback they need to keep improving their behavior. General statements like "You're so generous" or "You're so kind" don't offer feedback about specific behavior and may overinflate the deed. Children are motivated and encouraged by praise that matter-of-factly lets them know precisely what they are doing right. For example:

- "You used so many colors in that picture," instead of "What a great artist you are."

- "You kept most of your writing in the lines," instead of "Those letters are perfect."

- "You really kept your eye on the ball," instead of "You're an amazing baseball player."

- "Thank you for the cookies. You mixed the ingredients together so well that all the cookies looked smooth and were one color," instead of "You're the best baker."

- "Your story used so many new words, and when you had the cat sing upside down, I was surprised, and it made me laugh," instead of "You're such a talented writer."

Honest, sincere praise that is not manipulative or overdone can be a tremendous source of motivation and encouragement. Our children will feel affirmed by our praise and learn that self-motivation feels intrinsically good. Undoubtedly, they will be motivated to perform other acts of loving-kindness.

Wrap-Up

Moving our children toward true self-motivation is a challenging process. But this skill will have a substantial beneficial impact on their lives. Author and natural parenting advocate Peggy O'Mara wrote, "The way we talk to our children becomes their inner voice."

Even during periods of hardship, that strong, optimistic inner voice will help them move forward and motivate themselves. The correlation between motivation and achievement is formidable. So if we can establish the foundations of motivation early in our children's lives, hopefully motivation will become second nature. That is the goal, a lofty but priceless one—one that will directly impact both the joys and oys of our children's future.

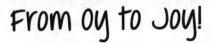

From Oy to Joy!

You'll know that you are moving from oy to joy when your child...

- stops asking you for help with basic tasks that she is proud to have mastered, like packing her schoolbag.

- looks forward to extended family gatherings and even helps you get ready by making signs or place cards or other decorations.

- takes on a project you never imagined he'd enjoy, like building a computer or learning to crochet a scarf.

- usually gets a reward for raking leaves but doesn't seem to care about the reward this time because she just wants you to see what a great job she did.

chapter 6

Nurture Kindness

"The world stands on three pillars: Torah, service, and acts of kindness."
—*Pirkei Avot 1:2*

"I've learned that people will forget what you said, people will forget what you did, but people will never forget how you made them feel."
—*Maya Angelou*

■ ■ ■

When educator Logan Smalley was bar mitzvah age, his mother made him volunteer at a camp for special-needs children. Logan admits, "I went kicking and screaming. But I ended up liking it (and the campers) so much that I stuck around all that summer and returned as a volunteer or counselor for seven summers after that." He ended up developing a strong friendship with a boy close to his age, Mario, who suffered from Duchenne muscular dystrophy (DMD), the most common fatal genetic disorder diagnosed in childhood. When Mario died at nineteen, Logan promised to look out for Mario's younger brother, Darius, who also had DMD. In the summer of 2005, Logan and Darius raised money for and took a cross-country road trip to raise awareness of DMD. The story of their seven-thousand-plus-mile trip to Los Angeles became an award-winning movie called Darius Goes West, which raised one million dollars for DMD.

■ ■ ■

Logan's mother, Barbara, knew that just telling her son to "be kind" was not enough. Kindness needed to be demonstrated through behavior. That's why she strongly encouraged (forced) Logan to volunteer, even though he resisted. And as many of us do, once Logan was forced out of his comfort zone, he discovered that his kindness mattered more than he could ever have imagined to Mario, Darius, and many other kids like them.

The concept of human kindness can seem abstract to children. It's not something they automatically understand or demonstrate. But they do know what it feels like to receive it. Kindness means being considerate, friendly, and having concern for others. It's the ability to turn the focus from ourselves and toward other people, making them feel valued and appreciated. Teaching this value to our children adds joy, depth, happiness, and compassion to their lives and, of course, to the lives of those on the receiving end.

This is easier said than done. That's why just telling our children to be kind is not enough. We must show them what kindness looks like in action and then give them opportunities to practice it. In Judaism, extending kindness to others is a mitzvah, not just a good deed but a commandment. Kindness is an obligation and thus should be our default behavior, something we do every single day.

Judaism provides us with guidelines for applying the principle of kindness to our daily lives. We are taught that the world "is built through kindness" (Psalm 89:3), and this includes most areas of life—from welcoming guests, to visiting the sick, to helping the needy. We are advised to pursue kindness in a deliberate way, and not randomly or as the mood strikes.

Has anyone done anything kind for you lately? How could you pay it forward?

The Torah was even accepted by the children of Israel with the words *Na'aseh v'nishma*—"We will do and we will hear" (Exodus 24:7). One interpretation of these words is that while we might "hear" what we are supposed to do, it's not until we actually do it that we truly understand it. The process of *acting* helps us to understand. So we must give our children opportunities to act with kindness.

Let's dig into some actions and behaviors that will help build the qualities of kindness and caring in our children. We'll explore four basic elements for infusing kindness into everyday life:

- Be welcoming

- Visit the sick

- Help the needy

- Perform deliberate acts of kindness

Be Welcoming

One particular story in the Bible shows us the enormous importance Jewish tradition places on hospitality. Imagine Abraham, sitting in his tent in the hot desert, recovering from his circumcision. In his misery, he notices three strangers (actually angels) in the distance. Does he close his tent flap to get the rest he needs to heal? No, Abraham rushes out to greet the tired, dusty men and immediately offers them a place to rest and food to eat. He requests that his wife bake cakes while he chooses meat for the guests. Abraham even personally walks with his guests when they leave, to see them safely on their way (Genesis 18).

Extending hospitality to others is deeply embedded in our tradition. From inviting guests over for Shabbat dinner to opening our homes for a Passover seder, we have many opportunities to perform acts of kindness by welcoming others. Our ancestors have taught us that we are really one extended family, and it is our honor, privilege, and duty to keep the spirit of warmth and generosity alive. Here are some ways we can do this in our families.

- *Greet guests eagerly and welcome them graciously.* Remember Shammai's suggestion to "receive each person with a cheerful face"? It's not just inviting guests into our homes that counts, but how we greet and treat them as well. Abraham had no idea that those tired, bedraggled-looking men were really angels, yet he greeted them royally and treated them with generosity and warmth. How do you feel when you're welcomed enthusiastically into someone else's home? Let's model for our kids how to greet and welcome guests into our own homes:

- Smile at them in a way that makes them feel valued.

- Welcome them graciously with kind words.

- Seat them comfortably.

- Offer them something to drink.

- *Put guests first.* Good hosts focus on the feelings and comfort of guests. Asking kids what they think would make the guest most comfortable, what might be the guest's favorite food, or what activities they might like helps them become not only good hosts but also kind people.

- *Be cheerful.* We are told that it is our responsibility to be cheerful when greeting and feeding guests (Talmud, *Derech Eretz Zuta* 9). Of course, it's smart to keep things pleasant and avoid hot-button topics (like politics) that could easily cause tension. It also is helpful before guests arrive to point out areas of obvious sensitivity (such as a recent death, illness, or divorce, depending on our kids' ability to understand and respond with sensitivity) that guests might have so they can be avoided. Our kids are part of the family team, and we need to teach our children (and also to model ourselves) how to be conscious of the feelings of others and considerate of what they might be going through. Everyone in the family should help make the time positive and pleasant. As parents, we can try to model this as well when our children's friends are visiting.

- *Participate in the preparations.* As most of us have probably experienced, food is one of the ultimate expressions of love. Many of our very best memories involve food and eating. When Abraham received the angels, the Torah intentionally points out that he ran to prepare food for

Try This! WELCOMING GUESTS

Escort your guests out! The Talmud records the importance of escorting guests out, praising one sage, Ravina, for walking another four *amot* (about six feet) on his journey (Talmud, *Sotah* 46b). Though this custom is little practiced today, it can make guests feel very special. When coauthor Maurice J. Elias was a child, he visited a family friend who always escorted his family out to their car whenever they left his house—no matter what the weather, no matter how far away they had parked. That host knew what Abraham, Ravina, and others knew: even at the end of a visit, guests appreciate being recognized and cared about, not just booted out the door so the host can get back to more important things. Seeing people to the door, at least, is an act of kindness in which we can involve even young children. By the time they're five or six, they'll love coming with a parent to escort guests to the elevator or to the car. Think how special you feel when people you have visited wave goodbye as you depart or walk you out. You likely have said to yourself, "What kind people they are." Join the club!

them. Not just any food—meat that Abraham selected himself. Preparing food and setting the table are great ways to teach kindness and consideration. Ask kids what would make the meal special—decorating the table or designating the most comfortable seats for guests. Even preschoolers can help you make a special cake, arrange flowers, plan an activity, or anything else they think the guest might enjoy. This will give them a little responsibility and ownership—and make them feel proud.

- *Be a considerate guest.* Judaism reminds us that hospitality goes both ways. It's important to be a good guest as well as a good host. The Talmud says, "The guests, for their part, should express their appreciation to their host and should not overstay their welcome" (*Derech Eretz Rabbah* 6).

Visit the Sick

The story of Abraham inviting strangers into his tent is about being welcoming and hospitable. But it is also about *bikur cholim,* "visiting the sick." The Talmud says that the strangers were actually angels, and they represented God, who knew that Abraham was in discomfort from his circumcision and wanted to show him compassion. When we teach and model caring for others who are sick or suffering, it helps our children to develop concern and compassion as well.

The Talmud tells us that visiting a sick person removes a sixtieth of that person's pain (Talmud, *Nedarim 39b*). While that percentage may not sound like much, to a person who is suffering, any relief is helpful and (hopefully) appreciated. It is critical that we tailor our response to the person who is sick or suffering. So although bikur cholim literally means *visiting* the sick, this mitzvah can be carried out through a variety of behaviors and actions, depending on what will most benefit the ailing person.

At times, though it may be difficult or inconvenient for our children to visit a sick person, we may decide that the benefit far outweighs any inconvenience. On other occasions, taking children to actually visit may not be physically or psychologically the best choice. As parents, we need to consider our child's age and emotional state, as well as the nature and circumstances of the sick person and their illness. If visiting is not the best option, there are many other ways we can show care and compassion. Making a phone call, sending a card, sending flowers, drawing a picture, or baking a tasty treat are all ways we can help our kids convey concern and love to the person in need.

Whatever actions we choose to care for the sick, Jewish guidelines for bikur cholim provide valuable insights as to how we can help our children develop empathy through performing this mitzvah.

- *Talk about positive, interesting things.* Maimonides, a physician, emphasized "telling [the patient] happy stories that expand the heart" (*Hanhagat Habriut* 2:20). Before visiting or calling, decide with your kids what might be interesting to the person who is sick. Small things that your children are excited to talk about are likely to be welcome conversation starters. Be sure to ask children what questions they have, and suggest questions that might be appropriate to ask the person they are visiting. Maybe find some news to share that could cheer the person up or make them smile. Remind them to try to focus on positive things and to not bring up anything that might be stressful.

- *Take something delicious to eat.* Because food can be such a comfort, Maimonides advises bringing food the patient can enjoy: "One should never forget to strengthen the patient's physical vitality with nourishing food" (*Hanhagat Habriut* 2:20). Of course, it's best to check beforehand if there are any dietary restrictions. By thinking about what food a sick person can and might enjoy, and then preparing it, our children can develop empathy and sensitivity to others.

- *Time the visit according to the patient's needs.* The rabbis of the Talmud caution us not to visit too early or too late in the day (Talmud, *Nedarim 40a*). If we visit too early, the patient may not be ready to interact and could be self-conscious about his or her appearance. If we come too late, the patient may be worn out and too tired to enjoy the visit. In other words, think about the best timing for the sick person and not necessarily what's most convenient for you.

- *Do small things that matter.* Rabbi Joseph Telushkin recalls a friend's grandmother who, when she was healthy, always had well-polished nails. During a long illness, her nail polish had worn off. Her grandson noticed this when he visited and polished her nails, something he was uncomfortable doing. Later, he learned that his grandmother told many other visitors that he had done this for her. Her grandson's small act had a great impact. Help kids think through ideas for small things that they can do, like fluffing up a pillow, moving the phone closer, filling a water glass, covering up the patient, adjusting the television, rubbing lotion on their hands, or offering to say a prayer with or for them. The point is to help our kids be alert to the small things they can do—with our permission and guidance—that will help someone be more comfortable and feel more dignified.

Try This! VISITING THE SICK

Plan ahead and bring along a shared activity. Visiting a sick person at home, in a hospital, or in a long-term care or rehab facility can be especially challenging for some kids. Consider bringing along a quick, light game that your kids can play with the person who is ill or with one another. Watching kids play and enjoy themselves can be wonderfully healing and distracting. Card games and dominos are especially good—anything nonelectronic is almost always better because it's easier to share and to create a communal experience. Bringing a game can also help children feel more comfortable and help them transition into more direct conversation and interaction with the person who is unwell.

- *If visiting is not appropriate, do something else.* There will be times when physically visiting a person who is sick or suffering is not the best option, even for adults. A 19th-century text on Jewish law counsels, "Be careful when visiting the sick that the visitor not be a burden to the sick person" (*Aruch Hashulchan Yoreh Deah* 335:4). On these occasions, help your children think through what act of care and compassion would be most beneficial and enjoyed by the person in need. Then make sure to follow up on whatever you decide.

Our goal is to teach our children that reaching out to a sick person is an important act of caring. When we model and guide them through these behaviors, we are helping them become more kind and caring people.

Help the Needy

The idea—introduced in chapter four—that we are all responsible for one another is one of the secrets to Jewish survival, and it's helped keep us together for millennia. We help the needy because it is our obligation and not just because we feel like it. In fact, the Hebrew word *tzedakah*, which often is translated into English as "charity," actually comes from the Hebrew word for justice, *tzedek*. We give to the needy because it's the just or right thing to do. Tzedakah is expected of each one of us, regardless of our income.

The twelfth-century scholar and physician Maimonides devised a "ladder" describing eight ascending levels of charity.

What do your kids know about your philanthropy? Could you tell them more about what you do or give, and why?

This ladder can help us learn to consider other people's feelings, put ourselves in their shoes, and then take action to meet their needs. Each step up the ladder brings us closer to meeting the other person's needs. The higher we climb, the more the recipient benefits and the more our kindness increases. This ladder is a great visual aid to help kids think through what being kind really means, especially when it comes to empathy and compassion.

1. The lowest rung: Giving begrudgingly and less than is needed.

2. Giving cheerfully but giving too little or less than is appropriate.

3. Giving cheerfully and sufficiently but only after being asked.

4. Giving to the other person before being asked.

5. Giving when you do not know who is benefiting, but the recipient knows your identity.

6. Giving when you know who is benefiting, but the recipient does not know your identity.

7. Giving when neither you nor the recipient is aware of each other's identity.

8. The highest rung: Giving whatever it takes (money, time, a job, other resources) to enable an individual to become self-sufficient.

We can use this ladder as a model when we talk about giving with our children. Discuss with them how, when, and why they can give and in what way the recipient will benefit, along with the ways in which receiving "charity" could make the recipient feel disgraced or embarrassed. The following questions may help prompt conversation and a deeper understanding:

- *"How can we put our money to the best use?"* We can help children learn ways to give effectively. This takes time, insight, and discussion. Examine what the real needs of the recipient are and how you can use your resources to help him or her in the short and long term. The top rung of Maimonides's ladder tells us that it's best to help a person in a way that enables him to become independent and take care of himself. As the expression goes, "Give a man a fish and you feed him for a day. Teach a man to fish and you feed him for a lifetime." Specific examples might be buying merchandise produced by people in need, donating to a scholarship fund, donating clothes to poor people who are job hunting, or supporting micro-financing (small business start-up loans to people living in poverty). Of course this level of giving is not always possible, and it may be more appropriate to step down a rung to a more practical level (giving gifts of food, money, or even toys) to help the recipient get through a difficult time.

- *"When should our family give?"* One way that nationally known storyteller Eva Grayzel makes tzedakah a normal part of her family's life is by keeping an envelope filled with one-dollar bills in a drawer near a tzedakah box in her kitchen. Whenever something special happens, to recognize the blessing and good fortune, the family takes a dollar from the envelope and puts it in the tzedakah box. Then, every so often, the family decides together where to donate this money. Every family can create their own unique habit-building activities based on their personalities, passions, and principles. Some families give before lighting candles at the start of Shabbat. Others set up a spare-change box (which can include dollar bills) and encourage one another to make deposits throughout the week. Establishing a routine for family giving helps build the habit in ourselves and our children. Remember that the behavior that gets repeated most often with positive results—through good feelings, knowing that the money will eventually do others some good—is what most likely will stay with our children.

Perform Deliberate Acts of Kindness

Think back to the story of Logan Smalley at the beginning of this chapter. His mother forced him to volunteer at a camp for special-needs kids when he was thirteen, and he ended up spending every summer at the camp (by his own choice) until he was twenty. Logan chose to give his time to the camp, and his parents supported that decision. Why do you think they did that? Because Logan's parents saw the tremendous value and importance of their son willingly stepping up to help other people and give to the community. They knew establishing a habit of helping would let Logan experience rewards that were not necessarily concrete but could be just as (or even more) life changing.

Getting a job may teach children responsibility, but volunteering teaches them empathy, caring, and community responsibility as well. And the intangibles can be substantial—humility, appreciation, self-control, sensitivity, pride, accomplishment, and more. When our kids freely give their time, effort, and resources to help others, everyone benefits—especially the kids themselves.

The Hebrew term *g'milut chasadim* means bestowing "acts of loving-kindness." This concept encompasses giving tzedakah, welcoming guests, visiting the sick, and giving of ourselves to help others. In fact, Jewish tradition tells us that performing acts of loving-kindness is even more important than giving money to tzedakah. The Talmud says, "Our sages taught: G'milut chasadim is greater than tzedakah in three ways: Acts of tzedakah involve money; g'milut chasadim can involve either money or personal service. Tzedakah can be given only to the poor; g'milut chasadim can be done both for the rich and for the poor. Tzedakah can be given only to the living—g'milut chasadim can be done both for the living and the dead" (Talmud, *Sukkah* 49b).

This last point is especially profound. We're told that the highest level of g'milut chasadim is escorting someone to the grave or burying someone properly. Why would this be so important?

Because a dead person is not able to repay the kindness, meaning that the kindness is given with no ulterior motive—it is pure g'milut chasadim.

True acts of loving-kindness are from the heart, not just the checkbook. They often take considerable time, effort, and personal sacrifice and involve helping in a deeper, more meaningful way. G'milut chasadim is an ongoing commitment, one of the deepest expressions of love. And it is an essential quality to model and teach to our children.

DEVELOPING AND ENCOURAGING EMPATHY

Helping people in need with a hands-on approach is a powerful way to develop empathy in children. Involving them in feeding the hungry or taking clothes and necessities to the poor will often put them face-to-face with those in need and make those people's situations far more real. Often, when children spend time with other children who are living in need (for example, at a homeless shelter or a food bank), they realize that those kids really aren't that different from them—people are just people.

Rabbi Lord Jonathan Sacks has pointed out that the Hebrew word *simchah* is usually translated as "joy" but that it has a unique extra meaning: "Simcha is joy shared. It is not something we experience in solitude." Our happiness and well-being are tied to the well-being of those around us. In a world often divided between the haves and the have-nots, it may be difficult to feel sympathy or compassion. What our children see in the world they are exposed to very rarely inspires genuine empathy. And empathy, at its core, is an emotional pull and not an intellectual one.

Hillel gave us great advice almost two millennia ago when he said, "Do not judge your fellow until you have stood in his place" (*Pirkei Avot* 2:5). When we act to help others, we can better hear and understand what their concerns may be. We can help our children become more actively and deliberately involved in understanding the feelings of those less fortunate than themselves.

When considering what to bring to others, let your children help by imagining what they would want if they were in the recipients' position. Don't let them dump a bunch of unwanted or leftover stuff from their closets. Instead, involve your children in selecting what to bring or do for others, focusing on what you're doing or giving and why. Similarly, when providing food, have children think about the best and tastiest food—food they would want to eat themselves. Talk to your kids and get their ideas about what people using the food bank might enjoy, what would be healthy for them, or what would be a special treat for kids their age. Then, when you're at the grocery store together, let your kids choose some appropriate items to give. One easy practice is having kids pick out one item for others every time you go to the grocery store together.

Remember to be sensitive to the recipients' pride and dignity. Being in a situation of need can be embarrassing or humiliating. The pain of their shame or loss of dignity is powerful, and we (and our children) must be empathetic. There could be fear, anger, resentment, and shame involved in this situation; often the response of the recipient isn't what the person giving might expect. The recipient may have a difficult time making eye contact or showing gratitude.

This is why g'milut chasadim can be challenging. It's hard for children to understand why people in need might be suspicious of our motives or might not accept help or express thanks at all. None of this should affect our willingness to continue giving, nor should it affect our attitude while doing it. We act because it's the right thing to do.

PERFORMING ACTS OF KINDNESS AS A FAMILY

The earlier we get started modeling this behavior for our children, the better. Helping others will seem easy and effortless to kids if it's just something that they've always seen and been a part of. Of course, if you haven't yet, it's never too late to start. Select appropriate activities for your children's ages; the opportunities and choices are numerous. You could:

- make cookies for people confined to their homes or in nursing homes.

- prepare meals for a homeless shelter.

- donate clothes, books, or household items to families or reputable organizations.

- write letters to kids with parents overseas in the military.

- visit pediatric units in the hospital to make friends, read books, or bring toys.

- help stock the shelves of a food pantry.

- write thank-you notes to or make pictures for local firefighters, police officers, and other community workers.

- clean up a broken playground or community garden.

These are just a few suggestions for opportunities to help others within our own communities. Remember the concept of values being "caught, not taught"—there is nothing that will help our children understand more powerfully than observing *our* actions.

Wrap-Up

Some of the actions mentioned in this chapter (like visiting the sick) might not be the first thing that pops into your mind when you think of building character and kindness in your children. But because developing character and kindness in our children has been important to Jewish parents and communities over the years, we are fortunate to have many shared values that help us accomplish this goal. This community expectation has held us, as parents, to a high standard and steered us toward doing the right thing even when it's the difficult thing to do.

Jewish wisdom reminds us that our children will understand through doing, not through lectures or demands, and certainly not through being shamed. The more we live our lives with g'milut chasadim, the easier these values will become and the more our children will model them, too. The point is to become proficient at doing things that make the world a kinder and more caring place for others. This provides a refreshing contrast to the mind-set of "looking out for number one." The biggest impact we can have in the world comes through reaching out to other people and helping them during a time of need.

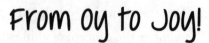

From Oy to Joy!

You'll know that you are moving from oy to joy when your child...

- does not try to get out of going to visit your cousins to pay a condolence call.

- adopts a cause she really cares about, something uniquely her own within your family, like banning land mines or protecting endangered species.

- actively makes his own list of what to bring on your next family trip to the food pantry or shelter.

- starts putting aside her money to donate—or even makes a new family tzedakah box to dedicate funds for a cause she cares about.

chapter 7

Cultivate Gratitude

"Today let us be grateful for the extraordinary gifts
and the endless possibilities of each day."
—*Rabbi Sharon Brous*

"As we express our gratitude, we must never forget that the highest
appreciation is not to utter words but to live by them."
—*President John F. Kennedy*

■ ■ ■

The mother of a preschooler was picking up her son before Thanksgiving break and noticed that the classroom door held quotes from all the students about things they were thankful for. Children had mentioned their moms, dads, brothers, sisters, pets, toys, and more. Then, she spotted her own son's quote: "I'm thankful that I can watch Noggin on television while I do my nebulizer."

As she read, she felt proud and thankful. Breathing problems and using a nebulizer aren't fun; even the most patient kids might have looked at those times as opportunities to complain. But her own little guy had somehow managed to set the negative part of it aside and find something to be grateful for in a less-than-ideal situation.

■ ■ ■

Have you ever tried to get your children to express gratitude? Of course you have; we all have. Sometimes, it feels like we're stuck on repeat, reminding our kids over and over: "Say 'thank you,'" "Remember to write a thank-you note," "Let's phone Grandma to thank her for the birthday gift." When we get tired of the hassle, we start to ask ourselves, "What's the use of even trying to do this anymore?" Then, because life moves so quickly, we can let teaching gratitude to our children fall off our radar. But that isn't in their best interest, or ours as parents.

Teaching gratitude is a difficult, continuous process that needs to be reinforced and revisited often because it's not something that kids can just be talked into doing. This is yet another concept that they can best appreciate and internalize through practice.

Gratitude means not only feeling appreciation but also expressing that appreciation through what we do. It is the practice of focusing on what we have, not what we *want* or think we *should* have. Consider that little boy in the story at the start of this chapter. Using a nebulizer, living with breathing problems, it would be so easy for him to become preoccupied with negative thoughts, dwelling on how things "should" be.

Gratitude is deeply embedded in Jewish culture, going all the way back to Jacob's wife Leah. When Leah had her fourth son, she said, "This time I will thank the Lord" (Genesis 29:35), choosing a name, Yehudah, that actually means "gratitude." In chapter one we shared a verse from *Pirkei Avot* that asks, "Who is strong? One who has self-control" (*Pirkei Avot* 4:1). The same verse goes on to ask, "Who is rich? One who appreciates what he has." At a time when power and wealth were the dominant values (perhaps the world hasn't changed much since then!), our sages recognized the ultimate value of appreciation.

So many people today are pursuing the best, the newest, or the most expensive of whatever it is that they have or want. All we have to do is to turn on the television to experience the consumer mind-set and the feelings of entitlement that dominate popular thinking. And this has trickled down to our kids, turning their focus on what they do or don't have, what their friends have, and what they see advertised. This attitude comes out not just in the form of wanting too many things, but also in their expectations of receiving them immediately.

Psychologist Robert A. Emmons, who studies the science of gratitude, has noted that gratitude has two parts. The first is an affirmation of the goodness that surrounds us, the gifts and advantages we've received. The second is recognizing that the good we experience comes from sources outside of ourselves— other people, God, the world around us. Recognizing this helps us feel grateful for the goodness in our lives.

But gratitude doesn't end there. Just noticing goodness isn't enough. Gratitude has a third component: it also needs to be lived. Feeling thankful is one thing; it's yet another to demonstrate gratitude through our actions. A study done by the John Templeton Foundation showed that as a society, we believe gratitude is important, but we are not very good at communicating it. This study revealed a vast "gratitude gap"—almost all Americans surveyed (90 percent) described themselves as grateful, but only around half (52 percent of women and 44 percent of men) regularly express gratitude.

Does it really matter if we feel and show gratitude? Absolutely. Studies in positive psychology reveal that cultivating gratitude can increase happiness and health. Giving and receiving gratitude also is associated with increased energy, optimism, and empathy. Jewish sources have understood this for centuries. Rabbi Lord Jonathan Sacks writes that when we give, "it is not just our contribution but we who are raised up. We survive by what we are given, but we achieve dignity by what we give."

In addition, research shows many specific benefits of gratitude. The habits described in this chapter can improve our well-being and our children's on so many levels.

- *Happiness.* Gratitude is powerfully and consistently associated with increased happiness. Doesn't that just make sense? Giving and receiving gratitude puts people in a better mood and helps them enjoy and cherish what they have. We can apply this to the past (positive memories and thankfulness for families, friends, blessings), the present (not taking for granted what we have now), and the future (living with hope and optimism). As our gratitude grows, so does the joy we will take in our children, our families, and our lives.

- *Resilience.* We talked about modeling and building resilience in chapter three. Gratitude, too, can strengthen resilience and help us get through difficult times. People who focus on the good are much less likely to be swept up into negative emotions. It's tough to feel both negative and positive emotions at the same time. So if we focus on the positive, we'll be much less likely to be overwhelmed by negative emotions. People with a grateful disposition tend to be more stress-resistant and bounce back more quickly from serious adversity, like illness, natural disaster, or other traumas. Of course, there will still be challenges, but hanging onto a perspective of gratitude will help protect our children against long-term anxiety and its negative effects.

- *Relationships.* Gratitude can strengthen relationships because it motivates people to recognize and appreciate support and affirmation from others. People who can freely express gratitude usually find that other people want to spend time with them because their focus is so positive, constructive, and encouraging. Being around grateful people tends to help us feel better about ourselves—and about them.

Freyda Siegel, aunt of coauthor Marilyn Gootman, offered a wonderful model of gratitude. Even at age one hundred, Aunt

Freyda was constantly making new friends, getting invited to one person's birthday party, another's Hanukkah celebration, a card game—a schedule that would have exhausted a woman half her age. One of the reasons she was so popular was that she was so much fun to be around. Aunt Freyda always looked on the positive side of life and never spent time complaining about what she'd lost. Instead, she rejoiced in what she had. There was even competition to be around her—over 130 people attended her one hundredth birthday party, with some even calling to request an invitation. Just imagine if we all could act like Aunt Freyda. What a joy!

Do some members of your family seem to give more and get less? Why do you think this happens?

Focusing on the good in life (even in the worst of times) is a cornerstone of Judaism. It's part of who we are as a people—we keep moving forward and don't give in to hopelessness. Think about the traditional Jewish toast—*L'chaim!*—which means "To life!" Rabbi Jack Kalla writes, "Jews appreciate every moment of life. It doesn't matter if things are going the way you want them, stop and pause, and raise your glass to the delicious opportunity life is giving you right now. You'll never get that moment back again." This is where Jewish tradition meets positive psychology, giving us very effective tools for parenting and for our family's well-being.

The Hebrew expression for gratitude is *hakarat hatov*, which literally means "recognizing the good." *Recognizing* means seeing something that isn't always obvious, a silver lining hidden in the clouds. While giving thanks is part of almost every religion, Judaism teaches us to be mindful and make gratitude a constant part of life and family interaction so that it will grow in our children's character.

One important Jewish tradition is to verbalize our blessings, not only on special occasions, but throughout our daily and weekly routines. Blessings—on food and drink, on special occasions or significant sights—are an eternal Jewish tool for teaching our children to practice gratitude. And by cultivating an attitude of gratitude in our children we give them a gift for life, which will comfort them and give them strength through good times and bad.

However, the busy pace of life doesn't offer a lot of time to pause, reflect, appreciate, or even feel the benefits of recognizing the good around us. So how do we move from having to remind our children to say "thank you" to instilling a greater appreciation in them? We want our kids to be grateful in a way that turns their thoughts from what they might not have to focus on what they *do* have. How can we guide them away from the false belief that they can't feel satisfied until every want or need is met?

Understanding the value of being grateful doesn't necessarily make it easier to act on it and then show our children how to do the same. Raising children to become happy, satisfied, appreciative adults involves helping them develop a daily practice of gratitude. In this chapter, we'll look at four specific practices that can increase thankfulness and close the gratitude gap in our families:

- Appreciate people

- Appreciate time

- Appreciate and respect the gifts of nature

- Appreciate and celebrate freedom

Appreciate People

When a six-year-old returned from a friend's birthday party, his mother asked, "Did you thank Sam's mother for the nice party?" To her surprise, he said no, he hadn't. When she asked him why, he explained, "The boy leaving ahead of me thanked her and she said, 'Don't mention it,' so I didn't!"

We've all said things like "Don't mention it," "No need to thank me," or "It's no big deal." The intention here is good—to show that we're happy to help one another. But our children may still pick up the message from these words that they shouldn't bother showing appreciation or thankfulness. Having things done for us and given to us is part of our culture of entitlement—after all, don't we *deserve* that kind of treatment? Not really. Oy!

Life-cycle events in Judaism give us many opportunities to express appreciation for the people in our lives. These are times when individuals are acknowledged and celebrated by their own family, and sometimes by their entire community. Together, these make up some of the most important practices in Jewish life.

- Birth, baby naming, and *brit milah* (circumcision) for boys or parallel ceremonies for girls

- Bar and bat mitzvah when children enter adulthood

- Marriage, when we make a commitment to building our own Jewish home and family

- Funerals, at which the life of a person is celebrated

- *Shiva* observances, to talk about the dead and comfort those left behind

- *Yahrtzeit*, a yearly memorial to remember a loved one

But Jewish practice isn't just about big occasions. We weave gratitude into the very fabric of our lives through traditions that help us demonstrate appreciation on a regular basis. We have already mentioned the many blessings Judaism offers on a daily basis. On Friday evening, during the Shabbat meal, we set aside time to appreciate our children with a blessing, as we mentioned at the end of chapter one. When we bless our children, it is a moment filled with joy, love, and meaning, which binds us together in appreciation for one another. Some families praise wives by singing or reciting the traditional Eishet Chayil, a section from the Book of Proverbs, which begins, "A woman of valor, who can find?" (Proverbs 31:10–31). Others add similar verses of praise for husbands, such as Psalm 112, which begins, "Happy is the man who fears the Lord."

All these types of blessings are meaningful suggestions for starting to bring gratitude into our families' lives. But the concept of hakarat hatov, "recognizing the good," also encourages us to focus on everyday opportunities. Think about the people in your life that you want to recognize and appreciate.

Appreciating people starts by modeling gratitude in ways that are clear and continuous. This comes in the small things we can do anytime to show appreciation for other people—a bus driver, a teacher, a cashier, a letter carrier, or someone who does work in our home. We can show our children thank-you notes we've written, count our blessings out loud, and talk about how we do good for others because good has been done for us.

Here are some suggestions for small, simple practices you can build into your family's schedule to focus on thankfulness.

- At least once a week, use dinnertime to have each person in your family—parents and kids—share two things from their day for which they are grateful.

- Model gratitude by verbalizing your appreciation—saying "thank you" to someone holding the door open for you, waving to acknowledge a driver who has let you go ahead in traffic, or telling a child, "Thanks for bringing in the mail so I didn't have to trudge through the snow." The list will grow as you start cultivating your skills in this area. And once you start verbalizing appreciation in front of and to your kids, they will start learning to do this themselves.

- Go beyond saying "thank you." When someone does something nice for you, do something nice in return, or "pay it forward" by doing something nice for someone else. Reciprocating kindness with kindness is the essence of hakarat hatov.

- Let appreciation flow—both to and about any person doing something nice for you. Tell your kids daily about what people have done for you (and what you have done for others). Work the topic of gratitude and appreciation into daily conversation and include topics like current events, public servants, and others in the community whose work may fall below your ordinary "gratitude radar."

- Don't forget to include your children in your appreciation. Don't assume they know what you appreciate about them; tell them. As parents, it's so easy to correct and point out what we'd like our kids to change—but we can cultivate the art of pointing out their strengths and what they're doing right.

- Write thank-you notes, and encourage your children to write them for gifts they receive. A personal, handwritten note really demonstrates appreciation, although even e-mails or text messages are better than nothing. If writing or time is an issue, at least have children call the person to express thanks and say how excited they are. Think about how you feel when you send a gift and hear nothing in return.

The twentieth-century rabbi Eliyahu Dessler observed that perfect love focuses on giving. He wrote, "The perfected world is one where every person without exception gives to and benefits others, and whose heart overflows with gratitude for what he receives from others."

As we've said here often, kids are usually more impressed by actions than by words. Take your kids with you and volunteer at a homeless shelter, a food bank, or a nursing home, as is appropriate to their age. They will see people reacting to them in ways that may make the concept of gratitude far more concrete. As we mentioned in chapter six, some individuals might not verbally express gratitude, but some will find other ways to show it. Pointing this out to your children as it happens is an empathy-building growth opportunity for them. This experience may also help you and your children feel grateful for what you have. And it could spark discussion about how it feels when people show or don't show gratitude.

Try This! APPRECIATING PEOPLE

We know it can be tough to feel grateful for people we're around all the time—like our family. So use a long road trip or another special occasion to get to know each other better. Break out a book like Gregory Stock's *The Kids' Book of Questions* to try out a range of fun questions about right and wrong, the things we value most, and how we'd behave in the face of a range of perplexing moral and ethical dilemmas. "What are you most proud of having done?" "What was the most embarrassing thing that ever happened to you?" "If you could take either a pill that made you braver or one that made you stronger, which would you choose and why?" These are just a few of the hundreds of questions. (Parents of younger kids may want to control the questions, since not all are appropriate for all age groups.)

Appreciate Time

Life has a way of demonstrating the wisdom that "time stands still for no one," even when we wish it would. We cannot contain time, whether we spend it wisely or recklessly, enjoy it or abuse it, live it fully or try to escape from it. Time always passes, and what is left are the memories.

Often, parents of younger children are told by older adults "Enjoy it while you can," "My kids grew up so quickly...I blinked and it was over," or "Make sure you're cherishing every moment." But advice like this can bring out mixed emotions: "Why aren't I enjoying this experience more?" You might know rationally that what they are saying is true yet be annoyed that they're no longer the ones sweating it out in the trenches of parenthood. So goes the constant pursuit of balance in parenting, trying to enjoy (or find joy in) one of the most difficult things we'll ever do.

Why do we so rarely stop to recognize time as a fleeting, precious gift? Sometimes, it's hard to figure out how to carve time for appreciation out of the fast pace of parenting. First of all, there's no precise or ideal way to appreciate time. It could mean special family time, one-on-one time with our kids, or just special moments of each day or week. It will certainly look different for each family. But if we take time to incorporate Jewish traditions into our family's life, we may find ourselves cherishing the smaller, everyday moments more. Writer William Arthur Ward wrote, "Gratitude can transform common days into thanksgivings, turn routine jobs into joy, and change ordinary opportunities into blessings."

APPRECIATE THE "FIRSTS"

Judaism has a traditional blessing called the Shehecheyanu that we use for "firsts," which acknowledges these as special moments that deserve emphasis and gratitude. The translation of the word means "Who has given us life," and it shows fundamental gratitude for the fact that we are alive to have new experiences.

This blessing is often incorporated into significant life events (major holidays, first fruits of the season, new clothing or a new home), but it is intended for much more. Any special moment that stands out is a wonderful opportunity to incorporate this tradition. We can say the Shehecheyanu the first time our family or child accomplishes something expected, like when a baby rolls over or takes a first step, or a child loses a first tooth. But it also works for days that are more momentous, like the first day of school or when a worrisome medical test comes back with good results.

What big "first" have you celebrated in your family recently?

We can also help our children say it to celebrate significant events in their lives, like the first time each year that they see snow (or, in a warm climate, the first time ever!), the first swim of the summer, learning to tie their own shoes, riding a two-wheeled bike, starting to read, playing a first song on an instrument, and every meaningful graduation from preschool and beyond!

Different families will take different approaches to saying Shehecheyanu. Some will say it freely and often; others will reserve it for what they see as major "firsts" and bigger events. The main thing is that each family finds a way to recognize blessings together and mark moments to be appreciated, both daily and on special occasions.

Using this expression of gratitude consistently will make it part of the bedrock of our children's character and behavior. The words of this blessing are:

Baruch Atah, Adonai Eloheinu, Melech ha'olam,
shehecheyanu v'kiy'manu v'higi'anu laz'man hazeh.

Praised are You, Adonai our God, Ruler of the world, who has given us life, sustained us, and enabled us to reach this time.

LOOK FOR BLESSINGS IN "DISGUISE"

In just about every Jewish prayer book, you'll find a list of blessings for a wide range of events, like seeing a rainbow, seeing the ocean, smelling a fragrant fruit, or hearing thunder. Jews also understand the benefits of looking on the bright side of things, even after a negative or emotional experience like illness or a brush with death. This is why Judaism incorporates a blessing that acknowledges times when we have made it through danger, such as a major illness or perilous travel. This blessing is called Birkat Hagomel (meaning "the blessing of bestowing [goodness]"):

Baruch Atah, Adonai Eloheinu, Melech ha'olam,
hagomel l'chayavim tovot sheg'malani kol tov.

Praised are You, Adonai our God, Ruler of the world, who bestows kindness on those who are accountable, and who has granted to me all kindness.

After hearing the blessing, everyone listening responds:

Amen. Mi sheg'malcha kol tov, hu yig'malcha kol tov, Selah. Amen. May the One who has granted you all kindness always grant kindness to you.

This blessing is recited in front of others in the community as a public expression of gratitude. To deepen the affirmation, the community responds with the blessing that the person receive only further kindness.

A Jewish folktale tells the story of a poor man who lived with his wife and many children in a small hut. The noise and crowding were driving him crazy, so naturally, he went to the rabbi.

The rabbi asked, "Do you have any animals?"

The poor man responded, "Of course! I have chickens, geese, and ducks."

"Bring them into the hut."

"Into the hut?" the man asked with shock and confusion.

"Yes, all of them, into the hut."

The man was skeptical but knew of the rabbi's reputation for wisdom. So in they all came! But with all those birds in a tiny hut, the noise was worse than ever. The man rushed back to the rabbi in desperation.

"Rabbi, the noise! I can't stand it! It's too much for me."

The rabbi stroked his beard thoughtfully. He asked, "Do you have any other animals?"

"I have a goat."

"Good! I want you to bring that goat into your home."

The man was dumbfounded, but what could he do? In came the goat. The noise got even worse, and the man, beside himself, ran back to the rabbi in protest.

"Rabbi, why on earth did you tell me to bring the goat into my tiny home? The noise is horrible, even louder than before!"

Again, the rabbi stroked his beard.

"Do you also have a cow?" the rabbi asked.

"Yes," the poor man replied.

"Good!" the rabbi said. "Bring the cow into your house."

Again, the poor man could only do as the rabbi ordered. Maybe there was some secret that the cow would add and all would be well.

Each day, the hut felt more and more crowded and more and more noisy. Finally, at his wit's end, the man went back to the rabbi.

"Rabbi, I'm losing my mind. With the cow in the house, there is no room to move, and the noise—oy gevalt!"

This time, the rabbi said, "Go home and put all the animals outside."

The man took off at a run, rushed into his home, and herded the cow, goat, and fowl out into the yard. That night the man and his family slept as they hadn't in years.

Well rested, the man went to see the rabbi the next day.

"Rabbi, thank you," the man said. "We have discovered peace and quiet at last."

"Always remember," the rabbi replied, "whenever you think things are bad, they could always be much worse."

The message of this story can be summed up nicely by an old Yiddish proverb: "If you can't be grateful for what you have received, then be thankful for what you have been spared." This story has been retold many times. For a fun, contemporary version that you can share with your kids as a prelude to a conversation about gratitude, try Bonnie Grubman and Dave Mottram's picture book, *Oy Vey! Life in a Shoe.*

Appreciate and Respect the Gifts of Nature

The Jewish calendar provides a year-round appreciation of the Earth. At mealtimes, we offer thanks for the land and the food that it produces. Why? From the Creation story in Genesis, we learn that we have a responsibility to preserve the Earth; it is not God's responsibility, but rather, it is ours. So it makes sense to respect the gifts of nature and care for the Earth.

CELEBRATING NATURE'S CYCLES

The Bible teaches, "To every thing there is a season, and a time for every purpose under heaven" (Ecclesiastes 3:1). Many Jewish holidays are agricultural festivals (though depending on where you live, holidays may not always correspond to the seasons in Israel). These holidays can deepen our children's understanding of the natural cycles of sowing and reaping and how important they are to our lives. Understanding how a seed is planted, watered, and nurtured before it eventually produces food helps children appreciate where everything they eat actually comes from.

The holiday of Tu BiShevat (the fifteenth day of the month of Shevat), usually in late January or February, is considered the New Year for trees and is marked by tree planting in Israel. It is the perfect opportunity to speak with our children about all the needs that trees fulfill, including food (nuts, seeds, fruits) and oxygen. Trees also reduce erosion, moderate the climate, and provide a habitat for many other species. Some Jews get creative on Tu BiShevat with observances like eating fifteen different fruits or holding a family "produce scavenger hunt" in the grocery store. Show your kids a video about the rain forest and help them understand the role of trees in different ecosystems.

Try This! APPRECIATING NATURE

For over twenty years, the first weekend in June has been the American Hiking Society's National Trails Day, celebrating over two hundred thousand miles of trails across America. Even if you're not near a trail, try to use this or another day to breathe fresh air and get out into nature with your family. Pick an activity to suit your own interests: hiking, biking, geocaching, tree planting, or water activities. Kids can help pick and plan the activity—and also take pictures for posterity!

In May or early June, the festival of Shavuot celebrates the gathering of the first fruits of the season—a great time to visit local farm stands or go berry picking. Allowing our kids to get hands-on and dirty helps build their appreciation for the hard work that others do to allow us to put food on our tables.

In the fall, Sukkot celebrates the final harvest. It's a nice time to enjoy visiting a local farm, go apple picking, or head to a pumpkin patch to combine learning about nature's cycles and the Jewish year with some family fun.

BLESSING THE BEAUTY OF THE WORLD AROUND US

As we've mentioned, Judaism offers many blessings to share our wonder and gratitude for the good things the Earth offers and the amazing world in which we live. These blessings are short, taking only a little time, but show deep appreciation for what is right in front of us. They remind us that we should not take for granted the beauty and awe of the moment.

Two very recognizable Jewish blessings show appreciation for bread from the earth (*hamotzi*) and for the fruits of the vine (*hagafen*).

Hamotzi (blessing for bread):

Baruch Atah, Adonai Eloheinu, Melech ha'olam,
hamotzi lechem min ha'aretz.

Praised are You, Adonai our God, Ruler of the world,
who brings forth bread from the earth.

Hagafen (blessing for grape juice or wine):

Baruch Atah, Adonai Eloheinu, Melech ha'olam,
borei p'ri hagafen.

Praised are You, Adonai our God, Ruler of the world,
who creates the fruit of the vine.

There are many other blessings we can say in appreciation of
beautiful or extraordinary things we experience in nature, such
as rainbows, which recall the covenant between God and human-
ity (Genesis 9:13).

Baruch Atah, Adonai Eloheinu, Melech ha'olam,
zocheir habrit v'ne'eman bivrito v'kayam b'ma'amaro.

Praised are You, Adonai our God, Ruler of the world,
who remembers the Covenant, and is faithful to the
Covenant, and keeps God's promise.

Or when you see the wonders of nature, like lightning or a
view of the ocean for the first time in thirty days:

Baruch Atah, Adonai Eloheinu, Melech ha'olam,
oseh ma'aseh B'reishit.

Praised are You, Adonai our God, Ruler of the world,
who continuously does the work of Creation.

The more we recognize and reflect on the gifts of the Earth
and its natural beauty all around us, the more our children will
learn to do the same. This appreciation will inspire our children
to care for our planet and its resources. It also allows us to share

the crucial message that every person has a responsibility to sustain it for future generations.

Appreciate and Celebrate Freedom

Don't all kids tend to believe that they're the center of the universe? This comes with a natural sense of entitlement and a desire for instant gratification. Who can blame them? Today, most of us take our freedoms for granted. For many children, times of oppression are distant memories or "just stories." So how can we share the true meaning of freedom with them and explore the idea that freedom comes not just with privileges but also with responsibilities?

We can help them connect the concept of privileges with responsibilities even while they're young. A three-year-old who stays in bed during nap time or at night has earned the freedom to no longer be in a crib. An older child who has always shown responsibility when riding her bike—wearing her helmet, following safety rules—can be allowed to travel farther afield or stay out longer on her own. Older children receive other age-appropriate freedoms as they earn them through responsible behavior and self-control.

Long before the Founding Fathers wrote the Constitution, the Torah told us to "proclaim freedom throughout the land for all who live on it" (Leviticus 25:10). Jewish tradition offers us numerous examples and teachings about the importance of liberty.

Several occasions during the Jewish year stand out as relevant and powerful examples of "proclaiming freedom." Let's explore ways we can use Passover, Hanukkah, and Purim to teach our kids the connection between freedom and responsibility.

LESSONS FROM THE PASSOVER SEDER

1. Retelling the story

   Recounting how the Israelites won their freedom from Egypt and established themselves as a nation brings an ancient story of freedom to life. Reflecting on the escape to freedom described in this story can set a tone of gratitude and appreciation for the whole night.

2. Reliving the story

   Many parts of the seder are designed to give children a sense—in a small way—of what it means to be stripped of freedom. We eat bitter herbs, which symbolize the bitterness of slavery; we dip parsley in salt water to symbolize tears shed by the slaves; we recline on pillows at the table to remind us that we are now free. Even eating matzah—which must be fully mixed and finished baking in less than eighteen minutes—symbolizes the Jews having to leave their homes so fast that they couldn't let their dough rise.

   We might ask our kids, "If we had to leave our home (forever) in less than eighteen minutes, what would we take? How would we choose what to bring?"

3. Living the story today

   Passover isn't just about history lessons. We can use this holiday as an opportunity to examine current issues and discuss ways that our family can work to free oppressed people today. The haggadah reminds us that we were once slaves, strangers in a strange land, oppressed and hopeless. We are expected to have compassion for those in similar situations today and work for their freedom. Organizations like American Jewish World Service offer wonderful materials on their websites to help integrate a modern message of freedom into the seder. There are even *haggadot* with modern themes of social justice.

4. Singing for joy and gratitude

   There is a lot of singing at the Passover seder, yet another way we keep kids actively participating. Throughout human history, singing has always helped people tolerate difficult times and express joy and gratitude after overcoming ordeals.

Among the most memorable seder songs is Dayeinu, a song of gratitude. Each verse recalls a specific thing God did for us and then proclaims *dayeinu*, "that would have been enough for us." But God did even more. We can explain to our children that singing Dayeinu is meant as an expression of joyful gratitude for our many blessings. After going through the traditional verses (of God taking us out of Egypt, of God giving us the Torah, etc.), your family could incorporate *dayeinu*'s of your own (like the end of a conflict in the world, Grandpa's recovery from a fall, or passing an important test or audition).

Celebrating and appreciating our freedoms shouldn't just be limited to Passover. But this is one of many wonderful opportunities around the year to make an impression on children and reinforce our blessings, especially the great gift of freedom.

LESSONS FROM HANUKKAH AND PURIM

Religious freedom also is easy to take for granted, except that Jews haven't always lived in a free society. Just as Passover teaches us about freedom from slavery, the Jewish holidays of Hanukkah and Purim remind us to appreciate religious freedom.

During Hanukkah, we celebrate the Maccabees pushing back their oppressors and rededicating the Temple in Jerusalem so they could be free to worship. While Purim is a celebration of the Jewish people being saved from annihilation, it, too, commemorates their being allowed to follow their religion freely. On both holidays, we express joy and happiness by dancing, singing, and sharing gifts of good food.

The stories of Hanukkah and Purim tell of efforts to destroy the Jewish people because we were different. Both holidays can help us to begin discussions about diversity and the importance of appreciating and accepting people's differences. And we can use these messages to promote all kinds of freedom, including religious freedom.

One reason we light Hanukkah candles is to remind ourselves that it's our mission to be a light to the world, making sure that others are never oppressed because they are different. We have a responsibility to be a part of the movement that makes this happen. In the words of Albert Einstein: "The world is a dangerous place, not because of those who do evil, but because of those who look on and do nothing."

Wrap-Up

Gratitude means being thankful, counting blessings, noticing simple pleasures, and acknowledging all that we receive. If we can model and teach our children to delight in the miracle that is life and the abundance of what we're given, then maybe—just maybe—we can shift from focusing on what our lives lack to focusing on what is present and beautiful. How could this not make our family's life richer, our relationships better, and offer us more happiness and joy?

Gratitude begins as an emotion of appreciation, grows into behavior that expresses that emotion, and then ideally becomes a new way of thinking. Once we start looking for things to be grateful for, we might be surprised at how much we have been taking for granted. Judaism helps us cultivate the habit of focusing on the small (but important) blessings in life and of constantly looking for the good in all situations and circumstances. Even the gift of a new day is a fresh opportunity to bring gratitude into our present experiences. We'll never feel grateful tomorrow if we don't begin to cultivate gratitude today.

As Ralph Waldo Emerson said, "Cultivate the habit of being grateful for every good thing that comes to you, and to give thanks continuously. And because all things have contributed to your advancement, you should include all things in your gratitude."

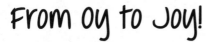

From Oy to Joy!

You'll know that you are moving from oy to joy when your child...

- sends his aunt a thank-you note without being asked—and doesn't wonder why he can't just e-mail or phone.

- thanks a store clerk at the mall without being prompted.

- spontaneously thanks a sibling for helping him carry a stack of heavy books up to his room.

- offers to clean out the litter box and then does it without complaining.

Inspire Our Children to Live with Integrity

"If you are not a better person tomorrow than you are today,
what need have you for a tomorrow?"
—*Rebbe Nachman of Breslov*

"Don't worry that children never listen to you;
worry that they are always watching you."
—*Robert Fulghum*

■ ■ ■

There once was a man who possessed a priceless ring. Its stone was a lustrous opal that refracted light into a hundred colours. But it also had the mysterious power to make its wearer beloved of God and of man. The man passed the ring on to his most cherished son, and so it was handed down, generation after generation.

Finally it was inherited by a man who had three sons, each of whom he loved equally. Unable to choose between them, he secretly commissioned a jeweler to make two exact copies of the ring. On his deathbed, he blessed each son separately, and gave each a ring. Each son believed that he alone possessed the authentic ring.

The man died. After the funeral, one after the other of the sons claimed to be the one to whom their father had entrusted his most precious possession, the ring. There seemed no way of resolving the argument because no one could tell which was the original ring. All three were indistinguishable.

Eventually they brought the case before a judge, who heard the story and the history, and examined the rings. "The authentic ring," said the judge in his verdict, "had the power to make its wearer beloved of God and of man. There is therefore only one way each of you will know whether you have the genuine ring, and that is to act so as to become beloved of God and of man."

—Rabbi Lord Jonathan Sacks, *The Great Partnership: Science, Religion, and the Search for Meaning*

■ ■ ■

We've covered a lot of ground in this book, addressing challenges that parents have struggled with from the beginning of civilization through the wisdom of our ancient religious tradition. We have explored respect, routines, resilience, responsibility, motivation, kindness, and gratitude.

Is that enough? Is there anything else we can or should be doing to help our children become the wonderful people we dream they will be?

Yes there is, and it's a priceless, precious aspect of parenting called inspiration. *Inspiring* is simply doing or being something that makes someone want to do, be, or create something praiseworthy of his or her own. Inspiration can offer deeper fulfillment and satisfaction. Inspiration involves evoking meaningful and powerful emotions that appeal to the heart and soul of other people. These emotions move people to act in a way that advances them and the people around them. Don't we all deeply desire to inspire our children to be loving, to be kind, to have self-confidence, to help others, to make the world a better place?

Parenting, with all of its joys and oys, is like that authentic ring. It is an amazing gift. The activity of raising and molding children can make everything else we do pale in comparison. We have the privilege—and the responsibility—of sharing with our children not only the values and traits to thrive in this world, but also the inspiration to act in a way that makes them beloved by God and other people.

To accomplish this final step of inspiring our children, we need to live *our* lives with integrity. We need to create an atmosphere that motivates our children. We can do this through the causes we support, the values we talk about and live every day, the books and media we expose our kids to, the people with whom we associate and whom we bring into our homes, and the way we treat them and others. All of these behaviors impact our children's developing character. And they all have the potential to steer their choices and, ultimately, their integrity.

We all hope our children will grow up to benefit themselves, their families, their immediate community, and the wider world around them. But they must *want* this for themselves because ultimately, we cannot do it for them. With the insight and wisdom of Jewish tradition, we can come closer to realizing this goal.

Such lofty parenting aspirations seem especially daunting in our overscheduled, high-tech world. This is why these proven elements of our tradition are even more essential today. Judaism provides the framework to carry out the seemingly small, but important, tasks. Our traditions teach us to take a moment to appreciate and give thanks for the food we eat and for our freedom, to take good care of our pets, and to welcome guests into our home. They also give us more explicit guidance, like planning a weekly meal together as a family, visiting the sick and lonely, or actively taking part in our community.

But this isn't just about Judaism or even just about religion. The wisdom and insights we have shared are relevant to any family, regardless of their beliefs. They tap into our greatest and deepest sources of continuing joy (despite the occasional "oy"): our children and grandchildren. Their truth extends across cultures, faiths, and history.

Bringing It All Together

Our journey has led us through a number of ideas and practices. Together, these will help us raise a *mensch*, a person of admirable character and good heart. When we give children clear and consistent messages about what is most important (through what we say and what we do), they are more likely to be inspired to act on those values—and to become adults who draw on the rich and enduring principles of Judaism to build a meaningful and fulfilling life.

Parenting is a journey of love, community, tradition, and principles. It is also one of the hardest things you will ever do. It brings with it difficult, stressful, and challenging moments. But the joy; oh, the joy, of raising children who make the world a better place. We leave our mark on this world through the legacy of our children. Let's make it beautiful. Let's make it matter. As parents, we can have no greater source of joy.

Discussion Guide

Discussion groups can be safe spaces in which we learn about raising children, share and test ideas, and help each other based on our varied experiences.

This guide is designed to help parents, along with grandparents, foster parents, stepparents, and others raising children, come together for group discussion, letting them reflect on their own current practices and come away with new ideas from other parents, centered around and inspired by ideas from this book. Your discussion group may be small or large, and might meet only once or over multiple sessions. Your setting might be a synagogue, a private home, or some other available space. We've created this guide to be as flexible as possible, so it can be adapted to your format, participants' knowledge, and time available.

Within each session, you may find it useful to use different strategies to encourage fresh dialogue. At different points, you might try splitting participants up into small groups and having two or three people exchange ideas ("pair-shares"), brainstorming and writing ideas on large flip charts or on notepads, sharing round-robin exchanges of ideas printed on index cards, as well as holding larger conversations within the entire group. Take note of which of these strategies work best for your group.

How you structure your discussion group will depend on how many sessions you plan to have. In this guide, we will look at a few possible ways of structuring those sessions, along with

THE JOYS & OYS OF PARENTING

questions and discussion topics specific to each chapter of the book. This guide covers the following topics:

- Planning Your First (or Only) Session

- Planning Further Sessions

- Chapter-by-Chapter Discussion Guidelines

- A Memorable Final Meeting Activity

- Handout: Live Your Life with Integrity Every Day

Planning Your First (or Only) Session

Whether this is the first session of a series or a stand-alone workshop, you'll need to adapt the discussion based on whether or not participants have already read the book. If you're planning to give out copies of the book at this session and participants have not yet read it, allow extra time so you can give a brief overview of what the book covers, and let participants read the introduction (along with, perhaps, the conclusion) before you break into activities based on the book.

It's always helpful to start by having participants introduce themselves with their names and the ages of their children (or grandchildren, foster children, stepchildren, etc.). Ask, "What do you most want your family life to offer your children?" to begin to generate discussion on topics covered in this book. Ask participants to share moments when they've experienced their greatest family joy, which you or they can list on a whiteboard or large flip chart; follow this with a list of things that contribute to their sense of "oy" as parents. This underscores the point that in transitioning from "oy" to joy, they are giving their children a solid, fundamental set of values and routines that will stay with them as they grow up, become adults, and perhaps start their own families.

Finally, ask participants what questions, concerns, or issues they have brought with them. Take notes and circle back to these as their concerns are covered during the session.

Throughout the discussion of parenting challenges and joys, bring in examples of Jewish wisdom (we've included plenty in each chapter!) as time-tested resources to help families become more peaceful and encourage children's resilience, responsibility, motivation, kindness, and gratitude—in other words, to help build a mensch.

Reassure participants new to the book that it will not require them to have any specific Jewish knowledge or practices in their own lives. Judaism offers a framework and an inspiration throughout this book, but all of the ideas here are applicable in any family, regardless of faith or background. Additionally, as we have acknowledged throughout the book, Jewish observances are not "one size fits all." Rituals and celebrations discussed here can be tailored to be comfortable and meaningful for any Jewish family.

If participants have read the book already, you can add a few of the following questions that may kick-start discussion in your group during this initial session:

- What are some ideas from the book that were interesting, new, or thought provoking?

- Did you read about anything that you are already doing or which confirmed your intuition?

- Did you read anything with which you disagree? Why?

- Choose one idea from the book that you would like to apply to your own life. How do you plan to do this? Did you encounter any ideas that you'd like to try but are not quite sure how?

If you will only be having this one session, think about adapting the material in "A Memorable Final Meeting Activity" (pages 236-238) to wrap up this session. If there will be future sessions, explain which topics you will be covering in future meetings, and perhaps offer participants a final thought or question to take with them and think through for the next session.

Planning Further Sessions

For additional sessions you can focus on one or more chapter topics, using the key takeaways, discussion questions, and talking points provided in this guide for each chapter. The length of your meetings will determine how many chapters you can cover at each meeting. In each session, leave some time for introductions, updates, refreshments, and other social activities. One hour might leave you about 40 minutes for discussion, during which time you can cover one chapter. With two hours, you can plan to cover two chapters (participants will likely need a break at some point).

One advantage of holding multiple sessions is the chance to review which strategies participants have tried since the last time and evaluate them, starting with "joys" and then turning to "oys." Helping your parent group become a source of problem-solving support for one another creates lasting bonds and gives parents resources they can turn to between meetings.

You may use the same basic structure for each further session, but vary the exercises to keep things fresh and creative, using some of the formats suggested at the beginning of this discussion guide, such as small groups, round robins, and brainstorming. Give participants time to talk, and keep a running list (either privately or on a large flip chart) of issues to come back to. Explore how these issues tie in with the themes discussed throughout the book, and think about how Jewish wisdom can apply in each situation.

At the end of each session, ask participants to collect examples of both joys and oys to bring to your next session. Both are valuable to hear about and learn from. Starting your sessions with these examples can create continuity and is a good way to recap ideas and principles discussed in previous sessions.

Chapter-by-Chapter Discussion Guidelines

To help guide your multisession meetings, we have listed a number of key takeaway points for each chapter, followed by a series of possible questions or suggestions that can be raised to create discussion around those takeaways. In the "Talking Points" sections throughout, you'll find more in-depth topics that could be used for an activity or deeper discussion.

CHAPTER 1: THE PEACEFUL HOME

Key Takeaways

- Caring, respectful relationships are key to a peaceful home.

- Good listening is a skill that can be acquired.

- The tone used to communicate sets the climate and dynamic inside the family.

- A peaceful home is not a place where no one gets angry.

- In a peaceful home, anger is expressed in a way that is safe and constructive.

- Problems are inevitable when people live together.

- Sibling rivalry is a natural part of growing up, but parents can take steps to minimize sibling rivalry.

Caring, Respectful Relationships

1. In which situations do you feel your children, spouse, or partner do not listen to you? Why do you think this happens?

2. How do distractions (of any kind—work, household chores, other children, outside issues) affect your ability to listen?

3. How can you set up situations so that you will be able to listen more carefully?

TALKING POINTS

Ask participants about the tendency—something we almost all do!—to carry on conversations while we're separated by rooms, walls, even different floors of our home. Why do we do this? What message does this send to our kids and to each other? It's definitely more convenient not to have to walk to where the other person is, but participants should discuss how this affects the ways we listen to one another. Even if we don't intend to shout, raising our voices constantly can have a profound negative impact on shalom bayit. Have participants brainstorm strategies to ensure more face-to-face communication and fewer raised voices.

Anger
1. How is anger generally handled in your household?
2. If you have more than one child, what are some different strategies you might introduce to help each one manage his or her anger effectively? One size rarely fits all!

Sibling Rivalry
1. If you have more than one child, what are some problems with siblings that come up in your home?
2. How do you generally handle sibling problems?

3. What are some new steps you've discovered in this book that may help you minimize sibling rivalry in your home?

4. The Torah includes many stories of sibling rivalry. What lessons do you think can we learn from all these stories?

TALKING POINTS

Have participants practice responding to the following scenarios using guidelines explored in this chapter.

- Your child stays out beyond curfew.

- You come home from work and find the house a mess.

- Two children are bickering about whose turn it is to do chores—each saying it's the other's turn. Or, for younger kids, arguing over whose toy it is.

Here are a few strategies that may be helpful: Find the feeling that lies below your anger. Try to use an "I message" to express those feelings rather than a "you message," like "I was disappointed that you weren't home by midnight" instead of "you broke your promise."

CHAPTER 2: ESTABLISH ROUTINES

Key Takeaways

- Schedules and routines allow children to feel confident and secure.

- A regularly scheduled meal, such as Shabbat dinner, refreshes and reconnects all family members.

- Routines create pleasant anticipation in our children's lives.

- Starting and ending the day in peaceful, predictable ways help our homes run more smoothly.

- Children are reassured by memorable traditions, especially those linked to holidays.

- Establishing new traditions gives families a creative way to take ownership and build rich memories.

Benefits of Schedules

1. What schedules and routines have you found helpful so far?

2. Which schedules or key routines are not working in your family's life right now (consider how you all start the day and get out of the house, gather for mealtimes, end the day)?

3. What needs to change? What schedules or routines would you like to try?

Rituals (Shabbat) and Regularity

1. Are you already having regular Shabbat meals with your family?

2. If you don't have Shabbat dinner together on Friday nights, how else could you introduce the concept of rituals and regularity to help bring your family together?

3. How are your family members involved in preparing the Shabbat meal? How can you get everyone more involved in preparation, rituals during the meal, or cleanup (at an age-appropriate level)?

4. What is something special that your family likes to do together regularly?

5. What are your family's favorite foods? Could you work these into your weekly family meal or Shabbat?

Memorable Traditions

1. What Jewish holidays do you observe?

2. What are some of the traditions you have established that you personally cherish?

3. Are there others that you wish you could add?

4. Do you use Jewish holidays and observances as ways to connect with extended family? Do you wish you could increase those connections? (There is no right or wrong answer here—sometimes, one or two family holiday meals a year is enough.)

TALKING POINTS

Ask participants: What are three concepts, perspectives, or quotes in your reading that you found interesting, new, or thought provoking? What have you read here that is similar to or different from the way you yourself were raised? Do any of these ideas tie in with the way you wish to raise your children?

CHAPTER 3: FOSTER RESILIENCE

Key Takeaways

- Resilience (meaning courage, resolve, and strength of character) is a quality that is learned and developed.

- Setting reasonable limits creates security and structure to help our children become resilient.

- Letting our children face hurdles and small disappointments without intervening can build resilience and help them face life's challenges with a good attitude.

- Through our own supportive listening and problem solving, we can help our children process setbacks.

- We help our children grow when facing disappointments by staying positive, embracing laughter and fun, believing that change is possible, and helping them set realistic goals.

The Importance of Limits

1. What types of limits do you set for your children?
2. Have you changed your children's boundaries as they've gotten older?
3. Which of your current limits do you feel are reasonable? Would your kids agree?
4. Which limits do you need to revisit if they're not reasonable?
5. Do you apply different limits according to the personalities of each of your children? What are the challenges in doing this?

Facing Disappointment

1. Think of one time you "rescued" your child from disappointment or failure. What could you have done instead?

2. Can you think of a situation in which you did not rescue your child, even though it was tempting? What was the end result?

Listening and Problem Solving

1. Think of a time your child experienced disappointment. Did you listen and help with problem solving? Did it help your child cope?

2. How could you do this better next time?

TALKING POINTS

Use the eight problem-solving steps outlined in chapter four (pages 125-126) to address concrete examples of how to help children deal with disappointment: your child not getting picked for a team, not being invited to a party, not doing as well as expected academically or in a performance; or even a family trip to an amusement park getting rained out.

How do your instincts say to react to your child or children in each of these situations? Using strategies from the book, how could you react instead?

Positivity and Fun

1. Can you think of a time when being able to laugh helped defuse a tense or unhappy situation?

2. When does your family have the most fun? Do you have any family hobbies?

3. What do you find funny, and how can you infuse more humor into your life?

TALKING POINTS

Dr. Benjamin Spock famously wrote, "Trust yourself. You know more than you think you do." (*Dr. Spock's Baby and Child Care*, 1945) From what you've read in this chapter or others, what are four strategies or practices in this book that confirm your intuition or reinforce the way you are already parenting? Does anything here confirm the way you parent but not the way your partner does, or the other way around?

CHAPTER 4: PROMOTE RESPONSIBILITY

Key Takeaways

- The first step in teaching responsibility (being accountable for one's own actions, acting independently, making decisions without anyone else's approval) is modeling it ourselves.

- Responsibility develops when children feel needed, appreciated, capable, part of a team, and aware of the consequences of their actions.

- Taking responsibility for mistakes has three dimensions (which we have called the three *R*'s): recognizing the problem, feeling regret or remorse about the problem, and resolving to take steps to solve the problem.

- Responsibility evolves as children grow, particularly as we give them opportunities to practice responsibility at home and in the community.

- The Jewish concepts of tikun olam (repairing the world) and bal tashchit (not destroying something of use to others) are tools we can use to help teach responsibility.

Modeling Responsibility

1. How can we model responsibility for our children? In which areas do you feel you are strongest when it comes to responsibility?

2. Watching you, what would your child say that you do to be a responsible person?

Cultivating Responsibility

1. When do you think your children feel most needed? When do you feel they seem the most capable?

2. How do you and your children currently show appreciation for one another and other members of your household?

3. How can we help our children express more appreciation?

4. If you have more than one child, what are some challenges each of them faces in the area of responsibility, given how different they may be from one another?

5. What teams are your children part of? How can you help them look, formally and informally, at their family, classrooms, and other groups in which they participate as "teams"?

6. How we can we help our children understand the idea of consequences without threatening or attempting to intimidate them?

The Three R's

1. What are some types of misbehavior to which we can apply this framework?
2. How can we help kids address misbehavior using this three-step problem-solving process?

Evolving Responsibility

1. What are some typical responsibilities you might give to children at various ages and stages of development?
2. How have your children's responsibilities changed over time? What do you think might be next for each child?
3. How do you know when it's time to revisit and change children's responsibilities?
4. What are some obstacles that might arise when giving a child more responsibility? How can some of these be overcome?

Practicing Responsibility

1. What kinds of community service or volunteering do your children see you doing? How do you explain it to them? How enthusiastic and positive are you?
2. How can you get your kids involved in what you are doing, even at home, and explain more about the organization or cause and why you're helping?
3. What are some options for children to help out in your community?

Teaching Responsibility

1. What are some practical ways your children can help to repair the world from an environmental standpoint? (Recycling? Gardening? Eating sustainable foods?)

2. Where is your family most wasteful, from the standpoint of bal tashchit? Can you and your child help brainstorm ideas for reducing waste?

TALKING POINTS

Lay out the eight problem-solving steps outlined in chapter four (pages 125-126) on a whiteboard or flip chart. Describe a situation in which you used the process to work through a problem with a child. Then, invite a participant to suggest a problem they are dealing with. Use the problem-solving process to help suggest some ways they could make progress. Participants may be more comfortable breaking up into smaller groups to have this conversation.

CHAPTER 5: SPARK MOTIVATION

Key Takeaways

- Autonomy, competence and confidence, and belonging play vital roles in self-motivation.

- When children feel confident in their abilities and competent in what they accomplish, they will be more motivated to take on new tasks.

- We can guide our children toward activities that will bolster their feelings of competence and confidence.

- Letting go (a little at a time) and helping our children set manageable goals help them develop self-motivation.

- How we express our disapproval can affect our children's motivation.

- Relying on rewards too often or for too long can undermine motivation by making the prize the incentive and not the internal satisfaction of doing something worthwhile; similarly, praise and encouragement should be used wisely.

Letting Go

1. Can you think of a time when you practiced letting go so your children could do something more independently? (Why is it so hard for us to let go?)

2. Can you think of a time when you didn't want to let go but did? What happened?

3. Can you think of a time when you wished you had let go but did not? What stopped you? What could you do next time when you are faced with a similar situation?

4. What are some ways we can help our children develop autonomy while still providing support and encouragement? What has been helpful to you so far?

Confidence, Competence, and Motivation

1. What are each of your children's strengths? How do you encourage them to develop these strengths?

2. What are some areas in which each of your children is trying to develop greater competence? What are their individual struggles?

3. How can you encourage them without stepping in too much?

Setting Manageable Goals

1. Do you have household goals tailored to each family member's ability?

2. Do your children set goals themselves for school or extra-curricular activities?

3. How can we help our children set reasonable goals, which are not too difficult, but not too easy to attain, either?

4. Do you feel your expectations for your children are fair? Realistic? Would your children agree? If not, what do you think needs to change?

Expressing Disapproval Constructively

1. Can you think of a time when you unintentionally discouraged your child? How did you do this?

2. How could you have reframed your actions or your comments in a more constructive way?

Guiding Children toward Success

1. How can you help each of your children spend time in areas in which they are competent, rather than always trying to master skills they don't have?

2. How do you help kids balance focusing on their strengths while being well-rounded?

3. What activities could set your children up for success?

4. How can you offer new and challenging opportunities so that children focus on good effort as well as success?

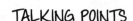

TALKING POINTS

Try to make a "map" of your personal and professional connections to others. With whom do you speak, communicate online, meet, visit, or work? At home, share the map with your children and help them make their own. See what connections they don't have that they might like to have. Often, mapping like this reveals examples of people we care about but don't communicate with as much as we would like, and others we communicate and spend a lot more time with than is really necessary.

Overreliance on Rewards

1. Have you ever been in a situation where rewards have squelched your motivation? Can you think of a time this phenomenon affected your kids?
2. What effect have rewards had on your children's behavior?
3. Which types of rewards have had the best long-term impact on each of your children?

Using Praise and Encouragement

1. Can you think of a time when praising your child backfired or did not have the intended effect?
2. Think of dialogue you've overheard between other parents and their children. Can you think of an example of exaggerated praise? What was the child's response?

TALKING POINTS

What are three ideas you read in this or any other chapter to which you found yourself having an emotional reaction, either positive or negative (surprise, embarrassment, annoyance, pride, etc.)? Why do you think those particular concepts resonated in this way?

CHAPTER 6: NURTURE KINDNESS

Key Takeaways

- Kindness is the ability to turn the focus from ourselves toward another person in a way that makes him or her feel valued and appreciated.

- Children have a very abstract view of kindness, so putting the principle into action, not just words, teaches children to be kind.

- Three important ways to teach children kindness are offering hospitality, reaching out to sick people, and helping the needy.

- Kindness in all forms requires empathy, and acts of kindness must be performed with sensitivity and awareness of the recipient's needs.

- Performing acts of kindness as a family ensures that our values of kindness are "caught, not taught."

Defining Kindness

1. What does kindness look like to you? What about to your kids? (Consider asking them for their definitions, sharing your own, and having a conversation about kindness, perhaps during a family dinner.)

2. The Torah is full of examples of kindness. What can these examples teach us about how to live our own lives and how to treat those around us?

Acting Kind

1. What are one or two little ways members of your family show kindness to one another?

2. Do you recognize these, or are they overlooked in the hectic pace of everyday life?

3. How could you start recognizing some of these small kindnesses in the future?

Hospitality

1. Do you let your children know when you are planning to have guests?

2. How can you get kids more involved? (Some suggestions: greet guests eagerly and welcome them graciously; prioritize the feelings and comfort of guests; be cheerful; help prepare and serve food and beverages; help with setup and cleanup.)

3. This chapter relates one coauthor's memories of a family friend who escorted guests out no matter what the weather, no matter how far away they had parked. What

is one way your family could go "above and beyond" in your hospitality?

Visiting the Sick

1. How do you reach out to family members and friends who are ill? Are your children involved in this?
2. Do you reach out to others who are hospitalized or homebound?
3. Based on the guidelines in this chapter, how would you decide whether to visit or simply phone or send a card?
4. What would it take (such as bringing a game along) to have your children join you?
5. How could you prepare them for such a visit using this chapter's guidelines?

Helping the Needy

1. What do your children know about your philanthropy, both in terms of financial donations and giving your time for different causes?
2. Have you ever explained to them how you decide which causes to contribute to?
3. Which causes do you think your children care enough about to want to contribute? How could you encourage this?
4. How can you take advantage of holiday times to talk with your children about reaching out to help less fortunate people?

Empathy

1. In the movie *Lilo & Stitch*, the little girl, Lilo, says, "*Ohana* means family. Family means no one gets left behind." What does *family* mean to you? To your kids?

2. The Talmud (*Shevu'ot* 39a) says, "All Jews are responsible for one another." What does this statement mean in our modern age?

3. How might you praise and recognize caring, so your children can be more aware of it and its importance?

4. What is one way each of your children shows kindness to another member of your family? (If you haven't paid attention to this before, it's helpful to start informally tracking it now.)

5. Rabbi Hillel said, "That which is hateful to you, do not do to another. That is the whole law. The rest is commentary. Now go and learn" (Talmud, *Shabbat* 31a). What lesson does this teach us about kindness and empathy?

TALKING POINTS

In the quotation from *Pirkei Avot* (1:14) at the beginning of chapter four, Rabbi Hillel asks, "If I am not for myself, who will be for me? And if I am only for myself, then what am I? And, if not now, when?" These questions can guide us when it comes to kindness and empathy. Ask participants, "From what you've read in this chapter or others, what are some strategies or practices for making each part of this quote a component in our families' lives and values?"

CHAPTER 7: CULTIVATE GRATITUDE

Key Takeaways

- Gratitude (feeling appreciation, then expressing that appreciation for what we have, as opposed to focusing on what we want or think we should have) has many proven benefits, including happiness, better relationships, and long-term resilience.

- Most of us feel grateful often but express this gratitude infrequently. This discrepancy is known as the "gratitude gap."

- Hakarat hatov, the Hebrew expression for gratitude, literally means "recognizing the good," in others.

- Life-cycle events can help us stop and appreciate those around us.

- Judaism encourages us to bless and acknowledge special times and occasions, which can cultivate an attitude of gratitude in our children.

- We can also find both traditional and creative ways to acknowledge the gifts of nature and freedom together with our children.

Feeling and Showing Appreciation

1. When and how do family members show appreciation for one another?

2. Do some family members seem to give more and get less? (Being aware of this can help us make sure we don't take things for granted.)

3. How could you help each child express appreciation to people, both inside and outside the family?

4. How could you personally start expressing more appreciation on a regular basis?

Time and Special Occasions

1. What are some unique ways your family observes special occasions?

2. Do you have any special-occasion rituals you love that you think other families could learn from and enjoy?

3. How do you involve your children in planning and celebrating these events? Could they be more involved? Is there an event coming up that you could mark by adapting a traditional ritual or creating a new one?

Gifts of Nature

1. What are some ways your family appreciates the gifts of nature?

2. What is one new, fun way you could help your children recognize agricultural holidays, understand where our food comes from, and appreciate natural phenomena?

Appreciating Freedom

1. How do you bring the concept of freedom (ours and others) into your family's Jewish celebrations?

2. How can gratitude for our freedom help your family connect more deeply with observances of Purim, Passover, Yom Hashoah, Chanukah, or Independence Days?

3. How do you help your children learn more about others who lack freedom?

TALKING POINTS

Before or at the last session, ask participants to list four techniques they have learned that they can apply to their own lives right away or in the near future. Make this as concrete as possible.

Ask: Where and how will you do this? Are there any obstacles or roadblocks that you can anticipate? How might you get past them? What other resources might help you?

A Memorable Final Meeting Activity

Regardless of how many meetings you have, it's useful to end on a memorable note. Here is an activity that fulfills that goal and can be adapted in various ways.

Distribute copies of this quotation, found on the wall of Mother Teresa's children's home in Kolkata, India. Explain that you will share the final two lines of the quotation later in the session.

People are often unreasonable, irrational, and self-centered.
Forgive them anyway.

If you are kind, people may accuse you of selfish, ulterior
motives. Be kind anyway.

If you are successful, you will win some unfaithful friends
and some genuine enemies. Succeed anyway.

If you are honest and sincere people may deceive you. Be
honest and sincere anyway.

What you spend years creating, others could destroy
overnight. Create anyway.

If you find serenity and happiness, some may be jealous. Be
happy anyway.

The good you do today, will often be forgotten. Do good anyway.

—Kent M. Keith, from *The Silent Revolution:
Dynamic Leadership in the Student Council*

Ask participants to share with a partner which of these statements touched them most deeply. Have several participants explain which statement they chose and their reasons.

Next, ask participants to write one or two original lines in the style of the statements above, based on what they learned from the meetings. They can each write on their own or collaborate. Again, share these with the larger group as time allows.

Finally, show participants the last two lines of the quotation:

Give the best you have, and it will never be enough. Give
your best anyway.

In the final analysis, it is between you and God. It was never
between you and them anyway.

Ask participants how this final statement sheds light on raising children in these complex times. Perhaps this is a good reminder that it is a challenging task. We cannot be perfect, but we can strive to be true to our principles, to be as good parents as we can, every day, and to forgive ourselves when we are not able to do so. Above all, Jewish tradition guides us to understand that when we live our lives with integrity, we are taking the most important step toward raising a mensch.

Make copies of the "Live Your Life with Integrity Every Day" handout on the next page for participants to take home. Suggest that they post it on their refrigerator to help them remember and reflect on the ideas and values they have learned in these sessions.

Live Your Life with Integrity Every Day

Strive to:

Listen carefully

Communicate effectively

Express anger constructively

Be a problem-solving family

Minimize sibling rivalry

Create predictability

Celebrate Shabbat

Establish memorable traditions

Set limits

Cope with disappointments

Be positive

Know how to laugh

Nurture responsibility in the home

Take on appropriate responsibility

Practice responsibility

Take responsibility for mistakes

Let go

Build confidence and competence

Create connections

Encourage effort and accomplishment

Be welcoming

Visit the sick

Help the needy

Perform acts of kindness

Nurture gratitude

Appreciate people

Appreciate time

Celebrate freedom

Appreciate and respect the gifts of nature

Inspire our children to live with integrity

—From *The Joys & Oys of Parenting*, copyright © 2016 Maurice J. Elias, Marilyn E. Gootman, and Heather L. Schwartz

References

Brous, Sharon. "The Surprise of Living." *OnFaith* (November 25, 2010): http://www.faithstreet.com/onfaith/2010/11/25/the-surprise-of-living/968.

Cardin, Nina Beth, with Gila Gevirtz. *Rediscovering the Jewish Holidays: Tradition in a Modern Voice*. Springfield, NJ: Behrman House, 2002.

Covey, Stephen R. *The Seven Habits of Highly Effective People*. New York: Free Press, 1989.

Dessler, Eliyahu. *Strive for Truth. vol 1*. Jerusalem: Feldheim, 1978.

Dweck, Carol J. *Mindset: The New Psychology of Success*. New York: Ballantine, 2007.

Elias, Maurice J., Steven E. Tobias, and Brian S. Friedlander. *Emotionally Intelligent Parenting: How to Raise a Self-Disciplined, Responsible, Socially Skilled Child*. New York: Three Rivers Press, 1999.

Emmons, R. A., et al. "Counting Blessings Versus Burdens: An Experimental Investigation of Gratitude and Subjective Well-Being in Daily Life," *Journal of Personality and Social Psychology* 84, no. 2 (2003): 377–89.

Friasa, A., P. C. Watkins, A. C. Webbera, and J. J. Froh. "Death and Gratitude: Death Reflection Enhances Gratitude." *Journal of Positive Psychology* 6, no. 2 (2011): 154-62.

Froh, J. J., W. J. Sefick, and R. A. Emmons. "Counting Blessings in Early Adolescents: An Experimental Study of Gratitude and Subjective Well-Being." *Journal of School Psychology* 46, no. 2 (2008): 213-33.

Gershman, Sarah, and Kristina Swarner. *The Bedtime Sh'ma: A Good Night Book.* Berkeley: EKS Publishing, 2007.

Grant A. M., et al. "A Little Thanks Goes a Long Way: Explaining Why Gratitude Expressions Motivate Prosocial Behavior." *Journal of Personality and Social Psychology* 98, no. 6 (2010): 946–55.

Grishaver, Joel Lurie. *Building Jewish Life: Rosh Ha-Shanah and Yom Kippur.* Los Angeles: Torah Aura, 1987.

Grubman, Bonnie, and Dave Mottram. *Oy, Vey! Life in a Shoe.* New York: Apples & Honey Press, 2016.

Jackson, Robyn R. *Never Work Harder than Your Students and Other Principles of Great Teaching.* Alexandria, VA: Association for Supervision & Curriculum Development, 2009.

Jules, Jacqueline, and Melanie Hall. *Goodnight Sh'ma.* Minneapolis: Kar-Ben Publishing, 2008.

Kaplan, Aryeh. *Jewish Meditation: A Practical Guide.* New York: Schocken, 1995.

Keith, Kent M. *The Silent Revolution: Dynamic Leadership in the Student Council.* Cambridge, MA: Harvard Student Agencies, 1968.

Kennedy, John F. "451—Proclamation 3560—Thanksgiving Day, 1963." *The American Presidency Project* (November 5, 1963): http://www.presidency.ucsb.edu/ws/index.php?pid=9511&st=&st1=.

Lambert N. M., et al. "Expressing Gratitude to a Partner Leads to More Relationship Maintenance Behavior." *Emotion* 11, no. 1 (2011): 52–60.

Livingstone, Tessa. "How to Spoil the Pleasure of Learning." *Guardian* (London), April 22, 2008.

Mandel, Sherri. *The Road to Resilience: From Chaos to Celebration.* New Milford, CT: Toby Press, 2015.

Mogel, Wendy. *The Blessing of a Skinned Knee: Using Jewish Teachings to Raise Self-reliant Children.* New York: Scribner, 2008.

Payne, Kim John, with Lisa M. Ross. *Simplicity Parenting: Using the Extraordinary Power of Less to Raise Calmer, Happier, and More Secure Kids.* New York: Ballantine Books, 2010.

Rothstein, Caron Blau. "Jewish Routines for Children." *MyJewishLearning:* http://www.myjewishlearning.com/article/jewish-routines-for-children/.

Sacks, Jonathan. *The Great Partnership: Science, Religion, and the Search for Meaning.* New York: Schocken Books, 2011.

Sacks, Jonathan. "The Pursuit of Joy (Ki Tavo 5775)." *RabbiSacks* (September 1, 2015): http://www.rabbisacks.org/the-pursuit-of-joy-ki-tavo-5775/.

Sandstrom, Heather, and Sandra Huerta. "The Negative Effects of Instability on Child Development: Fact Sheet." *UrbanInstitute* (September 26, 2013): http://www.urban.org/research/publication/negative-effects-instability-child-development-fact-sheet.

Sansone R. A., et al. "Gratitude and Well Being: The Benefits of Appreciation." *Psychiatry* 7 no. 11 (2010): 18–22.

Simon-Thomas, Emiliana R., and Jeremy Adam Smith. "How Grateful are Americans?" *GreaterGood* (January 10, 2013): http://greatergood.berkeley.edu/article/item/how_grateful_are_americans.

Slobodkina, Esphyr. *Caps for Sale: A Tale of a Peddler, Some Monkeys and Their Monkey Business.* New York: W. R. Scott, 1940.

Stangenes, Sharon. "For Nancy Samalin, like most parents, it was one of the..." *Chicago Tribune,* November 4, 1987.

Stock, Gregory. *The Kids' Book of Questions.* New York: Workman Publishing, 2004.

Schneiderman Sisters. *Oy Baby! 2.* Craig 'n Company, 2005, compact disc.

Tileston, Donna Walker. *What Every Teacher Should Know About Student Motivation.* Thousand Oaks, CA: Corwin, 2010.

Urban Child Institute. *Data Book 2013: The State of Children in Memphis and Shelby County. Urban Child Institute*: http://www.urbanchildinstitute.org/resources/publications/data-book-viii-2013.

Wood, A. M., et al. "Gratitude and Well-Being: A Review and Theoretical Integration." *Clinical Psychology Review* 30 (2010): 890-905.

About the Authors

Maurice J. Elias, Ph.D., is a professor in the Department of Psychology at Rutgers University in New Jersey, a contributing faculty member in the Department of Jewish Studies at Rutgers, and director of the Rutgers Social-Emotional and Character Development Lab (www.secdlab.org). Dr. Elias lectures nationally and internationally, is frequently sought out as an expert in various mass media, and devotes his research and writing to social-emotional and character development in children, schools, and families, as well as Jewish adolescent identity development and Jewish education. He has written an award-winning weekly parenting column and conducted Jewish parenting workshops. He is coauthor of *Emotionally Intelligent Parenting: How to Raise a Self-Disciplined, Responsible, Socially Skilled Child* (translated into Hebrew and ten other languages), *The Educator's Guide to Emotional Intelligence and Academic Achievement: Social-Emotional Learning in the Classroom,* and *Urban Dreams: Stories of Hope, Resilience, and Character.* He collaborated with storytellers in the United States and Israel and with a prominent Israeli school psychologist to create a book for young children: *Talking Treasure: Stories to Help Build Emotional Intelligence and Resilience in Young Children.* Maurice is the recipient of the Joseph E. Zins Memorial Senior Scholar Award for Social-Emotional Learning and the Sanford McDonnell Award for

Lifetime Achievement in Character Education. He is a licensed psychologist in New Jersey and writes a blog on social-emotional and character development for the George Lucas Educational Foundation at www.edutopia.org.

■ ■ ■

Marilyn E. Gootman, Ed.D., is an educational consultant who has advised parents, teachers, and administrators throughout the country on successful strategies for raising and educating children. She has over thirty-five years of teaching experience, from early childhood to graduate school, in both Jewish and general settings. She has written books for parents, teachers, teens, and toddlers, including *When a Friend Dies: A Book for Teens about Grieving and Healing,* and is coauthor of *Thank You, Trees!* (Kar-Ben: 2013), which the *New York Times* called a "charming celebration of Tu B'Shevat." Frequently called upon by media outlets including CNN, MSNBC, *Newsweek,* and *Parents* magazine to share her expertise, she has become increasingly passionate about her work running a group for Jewish families in Athens, Georgia, where she lives. The group, which she founded under the auspices of the PJ Library program, has blossomed into a powerful community for parents seeking authentic ways to weave Judaism into their family lives. The experiences of those families, and of her own three children and six grandchildren, inspired her to write this book.

■ ■ ■

Heather L. Schwartz, M.A., is committed to the education of students from primary school through the university level and is currently working academically with student athletes at the University of Georgia. She has worked on social and economic initiatives promoting the education of girls and children's health issues in developing countries. Heather has a master's degree in international relations and spent years working with an international organization in Washington, D.C., supporting lending and development initiatives for South Asian countries. She has also consulted for an NGO involved with microfinance and human trafficking in Nepal and Bangladesh and has guest lectured on international development at the university level. Heather has held leadership positions in the PJ Library program in Athens, Georgia; the Athens Jewish Film Festival; and parenting groups in other parts of the country. She considers parenting her four sons to be her greatest privilege and is in the midst of the joys and oys of raising them.

■ ■ ■

Rabbi Kerry M. Olitzky is the executive director of Big Tent Judaism (formerly the Jewish Outreach Institute), the only national independent organization dedicated to bringing Judaism to interfaith families and the unaffiliated. He has been named as one of the "50 Leading Rabbis" in North America by *Newsweek*. A leader in the development of innovative Jewish education, particularly for adults, he has shaped training programs for clergy of all faiths, especially in the area of pastoral care and counseling in the Jewish community. He has done pioneering work in the area of Jewish Twelve Step spirituality, as well as Jewish gerontology, and is the author of over seventy books and hundreds of articles in a variety of fields. His opinion pieces are published in leading publications throughout North America and in Israel. Among his most recent publications are *New Membership & Financial Alternatives for the American Synagogue: From Traditional Dues to Fair Share to Gifts from the Heart* (Jewish Lights Publishing) with Rabbi Avi Olitzky, and *Playlist Judaism: Making Choices for a Vital Future* (Rowman & Littlefield). Learn more at www. BigTentJudaism.org.